# Scaling Up with R and Apache Arrow

Analyze large datasets directly from R. *Scaling Up With R and Apache Arrow* provides a guide to working efficiently with larger-than-memory datasets using the arrow R package. As data grows in size and complexity, traditional data analysis methods in R often hit technical limitations. In this book, you'll learn how to overcome these hurdles without needing to set up complex infrastructure.

You'll learn about the Apache Arrow project's origins, goals, and its significance in bridging the gap between data science and big data ecosystems. You'll also learn how to leverage the arrow R package to work directly with files in various formats, such as CSV and Parquet, using familiar dplyr syntax. This book explores practical topics like data manipulation, file formats, working with larger datasets, and optimizing workflows for data in cloud storage. Advanced chapters examine user-defined functions, integration with other tools like DuckDB, and extending Arrow's capabilities to work with geospatial data.

Written by developers of the Arrow R package, this guide is essential for anyone looking to scale their data processing capabilities in R.

**Nic Crane** is an R developer, educator, and general enthusiast, with a background in data science and software engineering. Nic is a member of the Apache Arrow Project Management Committee (PMC) and part of the team who maintains the arrow R package.

**Jonathan Keane** is an engineering manager with a background in software engineering and data science. Jonathan is a part of the team who maintains the Arrow project including the Arrow R package.

**Neal Richardson** is an engineering leader focused on building software that helps people work with data. He is a member of the Arrow PMC and one of the top contributors to the project.

# Scaling Up with R and Apache Arrow

## Bigger Data, Easier Workflows

Nic Crane, Jonathan Keane, and Neal Richardson

**CRC Press**
Taylor & Francis Group
Boca Raton  London  New York

CRC Press is an imprint of the
Taylor & Francis Group, an **informa** business

A CHAPMAN & HALL BOOK

Designed cover image: Jonathan Keane

MATLAB® and Simulink® are trademarks of The MathWorks, Inc. and are used with permission. The MathWorks does not warrant the accuracy of the text or exercises in this book. This book's use or discussion of MATLAB® or Simulink® software or related products does not constitute endorsement or sponsorship by The MathWorks of a particular pedagogical approach or particular use of the MATLAB® and Simulink® software.

First edition published 2025
by CRC Press
2385 NW Executive Center Drive, Suite 320, Boca Raton FL 33431

and by CRC Press
4 Park Square, Milton Park, Abingdon, Oxon, OX14 4RN

*CRC Press is an imprint of Taylor & Francis Group, LLC*

© 2025 Nic Crane, Jonathan Keane, and Neal Richardson

ISBN: 978-1-032-66320-3 (hbk)
ISBN: 978-1-032-66028-8 (pbk)
ISBN: 978-1-032-66319-7 (ebk)

DOI: 10.1201/9781032663197

Typeset in Latin Modern font
by KnowledgeWorks Global Ltd.

*Publisher's note:* This book has been prepared from camera-ready copy provided by the authors.

# Contents

# *Acknowledgments*

A huge thanks to folks who gave us writing advice and really helpful feedback on our drafts of this book, including Sam Albers, Carl Boettiger, Raúl Cumplido, Dewey Dunnington, Alenka Frim, Colin Gillespie, Stephanie Hazlitt, Jared Lander, Bryce Mecum, François Michonneau, Danielle Navarro, Antoine Pitrou, Brian Repko, and Jacob Wujciak-Jens.

# *Foreword*

## Foreword by Wes McKinney

Data science using open-source libraries in languages like Python and R has evolved from fringe use by academic researchers and enthusiasts in the late 2000s and early 2010s to being the dominant, mainstream approach for business and research alike now in the 2020s. There has been a similar shift in enterprise software development and server-side data processing, where, for a variety of reasons, work that used to take place mainly in compiled systems languages like C++ and Java is now being done in dynamic, interpreted programming languages that were previously reserved to more of a "scripting" role for automation and "gluing" together parts of larger systems.

The modern open-source data science landscape has developed organically out of many federated silos that did not collaborate very actively with each other. Some of this history predates what we now think of as the "big data" or even "AI" ecosystems that are taken for granted today. I couldn't do justice to all of the nuances of how these different programming communities developed. Still, it is useful to briefly consider how we got where we are today and how you came to be holding this book in your hand (or reading it virtually).

R was created during the early open-source movement in the 1990s as a free and open-source alternative to the S programming language, which had become popular for statistical programming in the S-PLUS product along with other commercial statistical computing products such as Stata and SAS. R became widely used in academia for research work (especially in statistics departments). After a time, it started to become widely adopted for data analysis in industries such as life sciences, insurance, finance, and many others. In the 2010s, this business adoption was accelerated by a combination of a fast-growing collection of high-quality open source add-on libraries and new integrated development environments (IDEs), which improved productivity and collaboration on large projects.

Python as a data science language had a rather different path. The first version of the Python language was released in 1991, only two years before R's first release in 1993. For many years, it occupied a Perl-like role as a dynamic scripting language for the Linux ecosystem. In 1995, Jim Hugunin created the first numerical computing library, Numeric, and over the next decade, a small scientific computing community worked to create open-source libraries that would enable scientists to do work based on Python and open-source libraries instead of using a commercial environment like MATLAB. Python's usability for statistics and what we now think of as "data science" was limited until the late 2000s when open-source developers started incorporating ideas from R and other languages into Python to create new projects providing statistical capabilities such as pandas, scikit-learn, and statsmodels.

By the early 2010s, businesses worldwide were making a massive push to incorporate data science and machine learning into their companies, collecting and processing more data than ever to create new data-powered products and features to become more competitive and efficient. This created a simultaneous need for tools and systems to capture, store, and process massive quantities of data and professionals with the skills to develop and maintain data applications. At the same time, cloud computing services became generally available, making it easier than ever for small teams to set up and manage extensive "virtual" application infrastructure, where open-source software rapidly dominated the more restrictive licensing model of commercial software products.

It's perhaps no great surprise that, given the urgency of this need for data systems and skilled data scientists, these new data teams chose to use primarily open-source software and, in particular, high-level dynamic programming languages that are streamlined for individual productivity and interactive computing. This investment in data science has led to massive growth of the Python and R communities. In 2008, R was ranked by TIOBE as the 25th most popular programming language, but by 2020 it had risen to 8th place. Universities saw the value of sending new graduates out into the world with practical skills that they could immediately apply on the job and responded by incorporating Python and R into their academic programs.

While the open-source data science ecosystem has been coming of age over the last two decades, there are similar stories to be told about growth and progress in the field of database systems and large-scale enterprise data management. Early database systems were the backbone of the computing revolution and the early internet in the 1980s and 1990s, and they similarly played an essential role in the nascent "big data" ecosystem that came about in the 2000s with the growth of the now-massive internet companies that are omnipresent in our daily lives.

Internet companies like Google and Facebook (now known as Meta) started collecting so much data that they needed to create physical data centers and new types of software to cope with the massive computational needs of their products and services. Google began to share some of the details of the systems they had built (such as MapReduce), which led Yahoo! to create an open-source version of some of Google's systems called Apache Hadoop. Hadoop helped popularize the idea and practice of "big data." One of the core ideas from Google's early papers, which was reflected in the Hadoop ecosystem's success, was the concept of decoupling data storage from computing engines. Historically, databases were vertically integrated systems that bundled data storage, computation, and query language (SQL) all into one, sometimes even in a physical appliance located in a company's server room. In Hadoop, data files are stored in HDFS, a distributed file system that runs on a cluster of computers, and then different compute engines execute against the data files stored in HDFS, writing their results back to the same file system.

Within a few years, the Hadoop system spawned a fast-growing collection of open-source big data projects that worked with HDFS. A number of companies were founded to help regular businesses adopt Hadoop and related big data technologies so that they, too, could collect, store, and utilize massive datasets in their business. Open-source technology like Hadoop would be used alongside a company's existing database systems, which might have included commercial databases like Oracle, Teradata, or SAP and open-source databases like MySQL and PostgreSQL.

The open-source data science and big data ecosystems developed in parallel over a significant period and without much collaboration and coordination. Many big data systems were written in Java or languages that ran on the Java runtime environment like Scala, while data science was increasingly happening in Python and R. By the mid-2010s, data scientists found themselves needing to build their statistics and machine learning applications on top of their company's big data platforms, and, to make a long story short, it wasn't easy to do that.

At the same time that the big data and data science ecosystems were starting to converge and overlap in the mid-2010s, we also saw a significant acceleration in the performance of the computing hardware powering companies' data infrastructure. Fast solid-state drives replaced slow hard disk drives, while networking performance connecting computers together increased by ten to one hundred times (or more in some cases). Similarly, computer processors (CPUs) became faster and more efficient, and they could support higher levels of parallel processing because the number of physical CPU cores increased significantly. The initial generation of open-source Hadoop ecosystem projects was designed for scalability so that processing large datasets was feasible, even if slow. In most cases, they weren't necessarily designed to use cutting-edge computing hardware efficiently.

By 2015, the need for improved interoperability of big data technologies with the data science world and more efficient use of modern computing hardware led to a simultaneous reckoning in the broader open-source community. How could we reconcile these language interface incompatibilities while making our software a great deal more computationally efficient? At the same time, we also recognized the federated nature of how different communities had developed (e.g., the Python and R developers had little collaboration or code sharing over the years). We wondered if we could create an environment where developers could collaborate and share computing infrastructure across programming language boundaries.

These questions led us to create the Apache Arrow open-source project, a new kind of project with the initial goal of providing a fast, language-independent data interchange protocol for tabular datasets. This protocol is now commonly known as "the Arrow format." Once we established an interchange layer that would enable systems written in Java, C++, Python, R, Go, Rust, or other languages to send datasets to each other efficiently, we could create fast, reusable computing libraries for Arrow to power our analysis workflows. We have begun to think of Arrow as a "development platform" for making more interoperable and efficient data processing applications.

This book teaches you how to use the R Arrow library, which is a product of all of this work that started almost a decade ago. In addition to providing you with fast, scalable computing capabilities, it is also a foundation for using other Arrow-powered data processing tools like DuckDB or DataFusion and any others that may be developed in the future. Arrow for R builds on top of a common C++-based library foundation also used in Python and Ruby, as well as many other open-source and proprietary systems that incorporate the Arrow C++ library. The authors of this book are some of the leading developers of the Arrow R library: they have spent several years creating a thoughtful and intuitive experience to help R developers level up their data processing capabilities.

As a co-creator of Arrow, I am excited for books like this to be written and to showcase the benefits of the work done by the Arrow open-source community. The tools within will serve you well and expand your use of R to work with large-scale datasets efficiently.

# 1

# *Introduction*

## 1.1 The problem of larger-than-memory data

Those of us who love working in the R programming language know how well suited it is for data analysis. R is great for working with tabular data, which is a first-class citizen in R, with a data frame API being an inherent part of the language. There is also a vast ecosystem of packages that implement statistical methods and other useful functionality, and various deeply enthusiastic communities have grown up around the language.

R also allows the creation of novel, expressive user experiences for data analysis. With non-standard evaluation (NSE), it is possible to design APIs through which users can type intuitive code that gets translated into what is needed to do complex computations. Notably, the **dplyr** package defines a "grammar of data manipulation" that allows users to write code that is both easy to read and write. dplyr helped make R accessible to an even wider audience and has inspired innovation in other languages as well.

However, as you start to work with larger datasets, you start to run into R's inherent limitations. R data frames are stored in memory, so the maximum amount of data which can be worked with at once is constrained by the total amount of memory on the machine running the code. R is also single-threaded, so it can't take advantage of modern multi-core processors. Even if you can fit the data into memory, you may find that your code is running too slowly to be useful.

Some options for speeding up R come with undesirable tradeoffs. You can rewrite your code to use libraries that parallelize operations, such as **parallel** or **future**. This solves the single-threaded problem, but they can significantly increase the complexity of the required code. You can also use a package like **data.table**, which is optimized for speed, but it also requires you to learn a different code syntax. Even so, these alternatives still work on data that fits in memory, so if your data is too large, you're out of luck.

Other options bring extra overhead. You could use a database or other remote service to store your data and then use R to query it. This solves the scalability problem, but it brings lots of extra costs: a database or cluster requires setup, configuration, and ongoing maintenance. In a professional setting, this could require asking for IT to get involved, adding additional challenges. There may also be additional monetary costs associated with the required infrastructure and time spent supporting it.

Sometimes, a database is the right solution. But many times, your laptop or workstation should be able to handle the data you're working with. Modern processors are quite powerful, and disk storage is increasingly cheap. What would be ideal is a way to work with data that is larger than memory while continuing to use familiar dplyr syntax right on our own machines.

DOI: 10.1201/9781032663197-1

## 1.2   The arrow R package

As we will show in this book, the **arrow** R package gives you that ideal. It allows you to work with larger-than-memory data directly from R without needing to set up additional infrastructure. It implements the dplyr API, which means that if you are familiar with dplyr functions, you can use those same functions with arrow and don't have to learn a whole new framework.

Using arrow, you can work directly with files in formats such as CSV and **Parquet**—a format optimized for reducing the size of files and doing fast data analysis, which we'll discuss in Chapter 4—without having to export this data into a different format first. Just point at a directory of files, write dplyr code against it, and when it runs, it scans through the data in chunks, doing computations without having to ever hold the whole dataset in memory at once.

Let's start with a quick example of querying a large dataset with arrow and dplyr. Don't worry too much about what the dataset is or how it works—we will explain that throughout this book. Just know that it is over 53 million rows and 311 columns of United States Census data spanning 17 years, split into 884 separate files that total around 90 GB when written as CSV.

How many people rode a subway or light rail as their commute to work in 2021? And how long does it take to query the whole dataset?

```
library(arrow)
library(dplyr)

pums_person <- open_dataset("./data/person")

subway_riders <- pums_person |>
  filter(year == 2021, grepl("Subway|Light rail", JWTRNS)) |>
  summarize(n = sum(PWGTP)) |>
  collect()
```

The answer is that 1.5 million people ride subways—and all of that about a second!

But there's actually much more to arrow than shrinking your big data problems. As we will see in the second part of the book, Arrow makes it easy and efficient to query data in cloud storage, such as Amazon S3 and Google Cloud Storage. It makes it fast to integrate with other query engines and databases, like Spark and DuckDB. And it facilitates collaboration across other languages and tools.

How does arrow solve R's larger-than-memory data problems? And why does it make it easier to plug different tools and systems together efficiently?

The arrow R package is part of the broader **Apache Arrow** project. To understand how all of this fits together, we need to take a step back and explore the Arrow project's origins and goals. If you're only interested in knowing about how to get analysis tasks done with arrow, that's totally fine, and we recommend skipping ahead to Chapter 2, which provides you with a practical overview of working with the arrow R package.

> 💡 arrow vs Arrow
>
> Sometimes people mean different things when they say "Arrow", so in this book, we use "arrow" or "the arrow R package" to refer specifically to the R package, and "Arrow" with a capital-A to refer to the Apache Arrow project as a whole.

## 1.3 The Apache Arrow project

The Arrow project began in 2015 as a collaboration between the maintainers of a number of big-data projects. Since that time, it has gained a much wider community of contributors. At the time of writing, over 1000 unique individuals have contributed to Arrow. Arrow exists under the umbrella of the Apache Software Foundation and is governed by its core maintainers, who work for many different companies: no one person or corporation controls it.

From the beginning, the main goals of the Arrow project were to:

- create an efficient columnar format for representing data in-memory, optimized for analytical workflows
- establish this format as a standard, which if widely adopted, would enable greater interoperability between different programming languages and systems
- advance innovation by creating a solid basis on which to build other technologies and reduce the need for duplicated effort

At its core, Arrow is a **specification** for how data should be laid out in memory. The project maintains implementations of that format in twelve languages, as well as additional libraries that provide useful functionality on top of Arrow memory. The arrow R package is one of those, which wraps Arrow C++ libraries that implement a query engine, file systems, and more. Outside of the Arrow project itself, scores of other projects use the Arrow format and libraries, forming an ecosystem of tools that can work together efficiently.

Why invest in establishing a standard? Why focus on low-level details like bits in memory? It would have been much easier to just write a faster data frame library, without worrying about how it fit with other tools.

The focus on standards comes from the origins of the project, grounded in the challenges and inefficiencies in the analytics landscape a decade ago. By the mid-2010s, many technologies for analytic workflows had emerged, all solving related problems but in different ways. For example, both R and Python had tools for working with data frames, but the underlying data structures and methods are not exactly the same. They are different enough that a library written for R data frames can't just be used on a data frame in **pandas**, the popular Python library. It was hard to use R and Python together on the same data. Moreover, developers working to improve the capabilities of their language were duplicating efforts.

Beyond data frame libraries, there also was a proliferation of Big Data tools. Projects like Apache Spark, Impala, and Drill built on the previous generation's tech stack, notably Hadoop and HDFS, and greatly improved the scalability and performance of analytic workloads. These technologies brought a huge number of benefits to their users, but the landscape was fragmented. No single tool solves every problem the best, and each implements their internals differently.

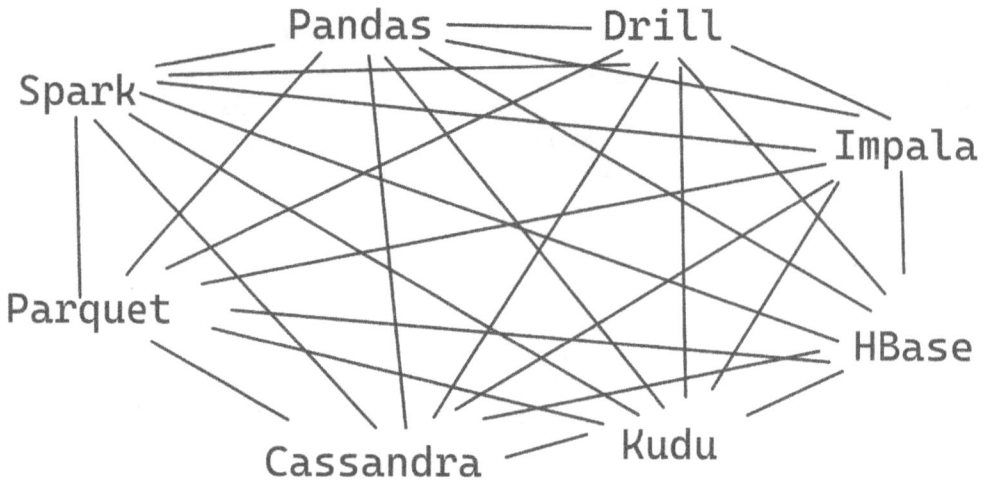

Figure 1.1: Without something like Arrow, you need an interconnecting component between each data systems

As long as you stay within one tool, everything is fine, but this is often not possible. For example, you may run a query in Spark, but Spark doesn't have all of the statistical methods available in R or Python. So, you have to take data out of Spark, move it across the network to your machine, translate it to the R or pandas format, do work on it, and potentially send it back to Spark for further work.

For developers, this is costly. We need special adapter code to map the data structures from one project to the other. And you have to do that special for every project you want to exchange with.

Even once those technical challenges are solved, there are performance costs at runtime. Converting data between formats takes processing time, and it can lose some details in translation.

Facing this scenario, developers from several of these projects came together and asked: can we define a standard for representing columnar data, such that each project only needs to implement that? Having that standard saves on engineering effort because there's just one adapter to write.

But in order to get the most savings, you also need to minimize the translation overhead. Ideally, the standard format would be exactly what every analytic project uses internally— then there is no translation. In practice, different databases and query engines make design tradeoffs to optimize for some use cases over others. So the goal of the standard is to be a common denominator, designed for general analytic workloads. This makes it close to what most existing projects were already using and desirable for future projects to adopt from the beginning.

What does that entail for the Arrow format? First, Arrow is **columnar**, like R, pandas, and most modern query engines. Many traditional databases and common formats for storing tabular data, such as CSVs, are row-oriented, which means that data is stored one *row* at a time, so values in memory would be taken from left to right and then top to bottom in the following table. This format is great for transactional workflows, where entire rows are

Figure 1.2: Using Arrow as a standard interchange, you need to only write one interconnector per system, at which point you can then use any of the other systems that also speak Arrow

being retrieved or updated, or extra rows are being appended to the data. However, it's less well suited for analytic workflows involving data manipulation, where we want to select a subset of columns, and perform operations like aggregated summaries.

Analytic workflows are better handled by column-oriented formats. What this means is that values from the same *column* are stored in sequential areas in memory, so values from a table would be stored top to bottom and then left to right. The result of this is that when the data manipulation task involved retrieving values from a single column, the entire sequential area of memory can be read, which will be faster than making non-sequential reads.

The Arrow specification is a columnar format and so is optimized for analytical workflows. Furthermore, implementation choices in the memory layout are optimized for fast evaluation and aggregation. For example, missing data is represented as a bitmask for all data types, unlike R, pandas, and NumPy, which use sentinel values that vary by type. Filtering by missing values, or checking if values are missing, is faster using bitmasks.[1] The Arrow string array is also represented in a way that improves the efficiency and speed of access relative to R and Python.[2]

Second, Arrow has a **rich type system**, encompassing all key data structures found across the database landscape, including many types not natively supported in R.[3] Bringing together the type system with the columnar data layout, we get the Arrow specification. Reducing it to its core, Arrow defines **Arrays**, columns of data of the same type. A dataframe-like arrangement of Arrays of equal length is a **RecordBatch**, which has a **Schema** that maps column names to the corresponding data types.

Libraries can then define additional abstractions on top of those core structures. For example, in C++ (and thus the R package) we have a **Table**, which can be thought of as a

---

[1] Wes McKinney describes the rationale well here: https://wesmckinney.com/blog/apache-arrow-pandas-internals/.

[2] This blog post by Danielle Navarro provides an accessible explanation of the Arrow string data type: https://blog.djnavarro.net/posts/2022-03-04_data-types-in-arrow-and-r/#character-types.

[3] See Appendix A.2.2 for full list of types and how they map to R types.

| year | location | age |
|------|----------|-----|
| 2005 | ny | 70 |
| 2006 | ny | 23 |
| 2007 | ny | 62 |
| 2005 | ca | 36 |
| 2006 | ca | 49 |
| 2007 | ca | 58 |

## Row-oriented

| |
|---|
| 2005 |
| ny |
| 70 |
| 2006 |
| ny |
| 23 |
| 2007 |
| ny |
| 63 |
| 2005 |
| ca |
| 36 |
| 2006 |
| ca |
| 49 |
| 2007 |
| ca |
| 58 |

## Column-oriented

| |
|---|
| 2005 |
| 2006 |
| 2007 |
| 2005 |
| 2006 |
| 2007 |
| ny |
| ny |
| ny |
| ca |
| ca |
| ca |
| 70 |
| 23 |
| 62 |
| 36 |
| 49 |
| 58 |

```
data | >
    summarize(mean(age))
```

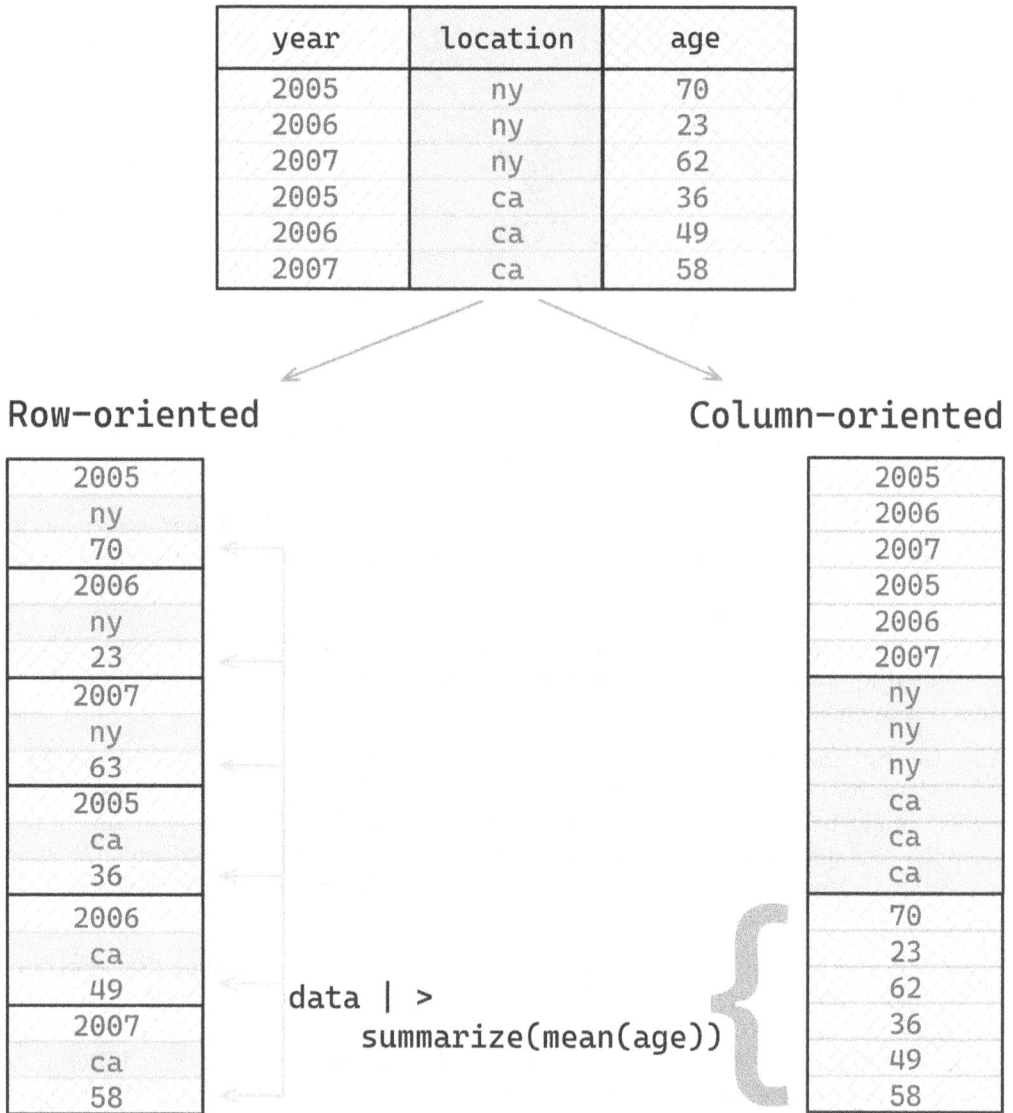

Figure 1.3: Comparison of how row-oriented and column-oriented formats store the same tabular data

data frame that is chunked into multiple batches, and a **RecordBatchReader**, an iterator that yields RecordBatches for processing. A **Dataset** makes a connection to a data source, such as a file or directory of files, and provides an interface to yield batches of data efficiently. These are the core building blocks on which high-performance data-frame libraries and query engines can be built.

The early years of the Arrow project were focused on developing the specification and building out basic implementations in multiple languages that projects could use to get data into and out of the Arrow format. The first significant proof of the value of Arrow as a standard came in 2017 with the integration between Spark (a Java project) and pandas via PySpark (using the Python bindings to the Arrow C++ library). As we will discuss

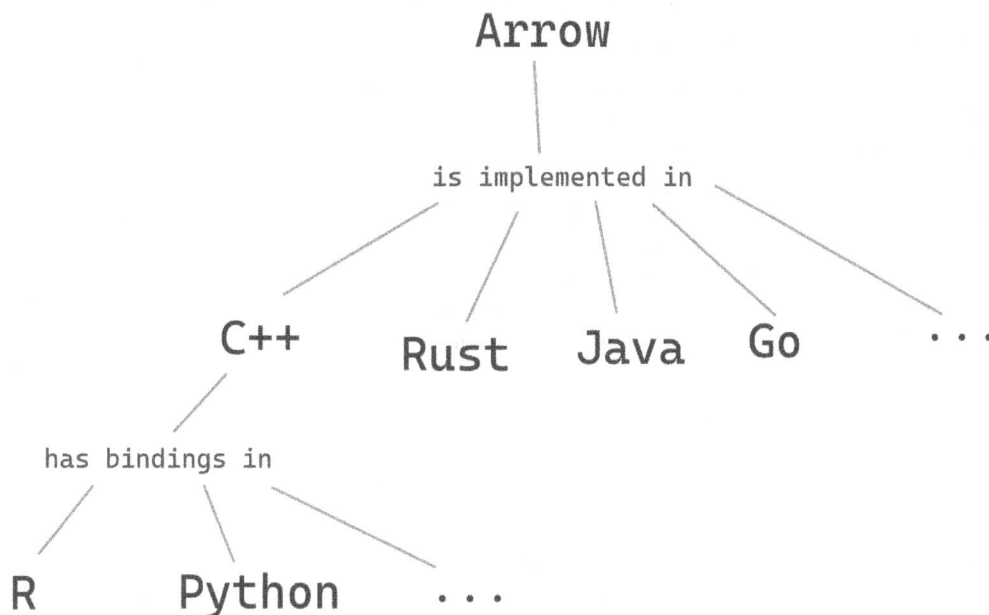

Figure 1.4: Implementation structure showing how the Arrow standard is implemented in a number of languages, and some of the higher-level language implementations like Python and R depend on lower-level implementations like C++

further in Chapter 8, using Arrow to exchange data demonstrated significant speedups in workflows that involved Spark and pandas together.

After the initial foundations were built, projects both inside Apache Arrow and in the broader community began building Arrow-native solutions. That is, Arrow wasn't just the means of exchanging data with others; it was the memory model on the inside. No translation is required when communicating between Arrow-native projects because their internal data layout is the same.

One such project is the query engine in the Arrow C++ library, called **Acero**. This is what powers the dplyr backend in the arrow R package, and we will spend a few chapters digging into its capabilities. We—the authors, along with others in the Arrow developer community—wanted to build a solution to the problems outlined at the top of the chapter. And we wanted to build something that demonstrated the value of the design choices in the Arrow format. If Arrow is a memory format for data that is optimal for analytic workloads, we should be able to build a high-performance query engine on top of it. And if Arrow makes integrations with other projects more efficient, we should be able to plug this query engine into other tools naturally.

The influence of Arrow goes beyond the specifics of this C++ library, though. Another project that grew within Apache Arrow is **DataFusion**, an Arrow-native query engine written in Rust. Other projects, like the **polars** data frame library, are built on Arrow but are governed independently. Still others, such as **DuckDB**, have an internal format that is nearly the same as Arrow, but with some different tradeoffs chosen. Projects like DuckDB are sufficiently similar in their implementations that it is possible to integrate them with Arrow with minimal effort so that data can be shared between Arrow and each of them without the need for costly copying back and forth. This translation cost is known as **serialization** and **deserialization**.

The Arrow format and specification is a key tool in the broader drive to create composable analytic systems. In a composable system, you can plug together different components that best meet your needs, rather than having to adopt closed products that include everything, from the storage layer to compute methods and the front-end user experience. Standards like Arrow allow you to integrate different solutions, such as DuckDB and DataFusion, that may be better at one thing or another, without the overhead of having to translate between proprietary data formats. As such, the value of Arrow in R goes beyond the specific capabilities of the arrow R package, with the ideas and philosophy being in some ways more important than the specific implementations themselves.

## 1.4   This book

In Chapter 2, we give an overview of working with arrow and introduce some key ideas and concepts that you'll need to know. Then in Chapter 3 we look at what you need to know about manipulating data using arrow and how most of the time you can work with functionality identical to that of the dplyr package.

The format of the data you're working with can have a big impact on how efficiently you can analyze your data, and so in Chapter 4, we explore the different file formats that you can work with in arrow and explain the crucial differences between them. Beyond choosing a good file format, we will demonstrate some specific techniques to optimize working with larger-than-memory datasets, which we discuss in Chapter 5. We extend the lessons we learned earlier about datasets and discuss working with data in cloud storage and specifically how arrow can help with this in Chapter 6. Not only will you learn how to connect with data in cloud storage, but you will also see how to query it optimally.

We go on to talk about more sophisticated techniques for data analysis, including user-defined functions and extending arrow to work with geospatial data, in Chapter 7. Finally, we take a look at sharing data within the same process, between processes, and across networks in Chapter 8.

# 2

# *Getting Started*

In this chapter we will introduce the package and the data that we'll be using in the majority of examples in this book. We'll also be introducing key concepts that we'll be going into more detail about in later chapters.

## 2.1 Installing Arrow

The arrow R package provides bindings to the Arrow C++ library, and so both must be installed together. Normally, you don't have to do anything unusual to do this, and, as with other R packages, Arrow can be installed by using `install.packages()`.

```
install.packages("arrow")
```

If you want to customize your arrow installation, you can find more information in the installation guide[1], though for the majority of circumstances this isn't necessary and the default installation will contain all the necessary features to work productively with arrow.

## 2.2 PUMS dataset

Many of the examples in this book use data from the Public Use Microdata Sample (PUMS)[2] from the United States Census. Although the full-country census takes place every 10 years, the American Community Survey is conducted every year and that PUMS data is what we use here. The dataset we have here covers the years 2005–2022. The raw data was retrieved from the Census's FTP site[3], with many values recoded and cleaned, so we can focus here on demonstrating arrow's capabilities.

This is a dataset that comes from a detailed survey that is sent out to a subset of US residents every year. The dataset is released for public use by the Census Bureau in a raw CSV form. We have cleaned it up and converted it to a Parquet-based dataset for use with Arrow for demonstration purposes in this book.

One thing we have to pay attention to is that this dataset is weighted, so we can't simply count the number of rows to get an accurate count of population—instead we sum or multiply by the weighting variables. This is why the example in the Introduction did `sum(PWGTP)`

---

[1] https://arrow.apache.org/docs/r/articles/install.html
[2] https://www.census.gov/programs-surveys/acs/microdata.html
[3] https://www2.census.gov/programs-surveys/acs/data/pums/

DOI: 10.1201/9781032663197-2

rather than just `n()` to count the population. We will discuss this weighting in our analysis below. If you want to know more details about the dataset, including how you can get hold of it, you can read more about it in Section A.2.1.

## 2.3   Opening the dataset

Let's take a look at the data in R. The data is stored in a directory called `./data/pums/person`. This is further split into multiple directories, one for each year, and then within those directories, one for each location. Finally, within each state directory, there is a single Parquet file containing the data for that year and location.[4]

```
./data/pums/person/
  year=2005
    location=ak
        part-0.parquet
...
    location=wy
        part-0.parquet
  year=2006
    location=ak
        part-0.parquet
...
    location=wy
        part-0.parquet
```

If we want to take a quick look at one of the files in the dataset, we can use `read_parquet()` to read it into R.

```
library(arrow)
path <- "./data/person/year=2021/location=ca/part-0.parquet"
read_parquet(path)
```

```
# A tibble: 386,061 x 309
   SPORDER RT        SERIALNO  PUMA   ST    ADJUST PWGTP  AGEP CIT
     <int> <fct>     <chr>     <chr>  <chr>  <int> <int> <int> <fct>
 1       2 Person~ 2021HU0~ 05918 Cali~     NA    62    48 U.S.~
 2       3 Person~ 2021HU0~ 05918 Cali~     NA    68    18 Born~
 3       4 Person~ 2021HU0~ 05918 Cali~     NA    61    15 Born~
 4       1 Person~ 2021HU0~ 03710 Cali~     NA    35    58 Born~
 5       2 Person~ 2021HU0~ 03710 Cali~     NA    38    54 Born~
 6       3 Person~ 2021HU0~ 03710 Cali~     NA    36    28 Born~
 7       1 Person~ 2021HU0~ 08513 Cali~     NA    80    71 Born~
 8       2 Person~ 2021HU0~ 08513 Cali~     NA    90    71 Born~
 9       1 Person~ 2021HU0~ 06507 Cali~     NA   120    38 Born~
10       2 Person~ 2021HU0~ 06507 Cali~     NA   119    40 Born~
# i 386,051 more rows
# i 300 more variables: COW <fct>, DDRS <lgl>, DEYE <lgl>,
#   DOUT <lgl>, DPHY <lgl>, DREM <lgl>, DWRK <lgl>, ENG <fct>,
```

---

[4]Unfamiliar with the Parquet file format? Don't worry, we'll cover that in Chapter 4

```
#   FER <lgl>, GCL <lgl>, GCM <fct>, GCR <lgl>, INTP <int>,
#   JWMNP <int>, JWRIP <chr>, JWTR <chr>, LANX <lgl>,
#   MAR <fct>, MIG <lgl>, MIL <fct>, MILY <fct>, MLPA <lgl>,
#   MLPB <lgl>, MLPC <lgl>, MLPD <lgl>, MLPE <lgl>, ...
```

Our full dataset is stored across multiple files. We don't have to worry about that though, as arrow can work with them as a single object, called an **Arrow Dataset**. To open the dataset in arrow, we use the `open_dataset()` function, and provide the path to the data. Arrow can work with data in multiple formats, including a range of delimited text formats like CSV, JSON, and the Parquet format—an efficient binary file format with support in many languages—which we are working with here. We'll discuss the different formats in detail in Chapter 4.

```
pums_person <- open_dataset("./data/person")
```

Now Arrow knows where our data is stored, so let's learn more about the dataset we just created. Let's begin by looking at its size. How big is our dataset in terms of rows and columns?

```
dim(pums_person)
```

```
[1] 53528050      311
```

It's over 53 million rows and 311 columns, which sounds pretty big. It's certainly more than can be loaded into the memory of most machines people use in their day-to-day work.

So how can we work with this data? When we called `open_dataset()` earlier, we created an Arrow Dataset object, which doesn't read all of the data into our R session. Instead, it captures information about where the data is on disk and some additional metadata. We can see some of this metadata if we print the dataset.

```
pums_person
```

```
FileSystemDataset with 884 Parquet files
311 columns
SPORDER: int32
RT: dictionary<values=string, indices=int32>
SERIALNO: string
PUMA: string
ST: string
ADJUST: int32
PWGTP: int32
AGEP: int32
CIT: dictionary<values=string, indices=int32>
COW: dictionary<values=string, indices=int32>
DDRS: bool
DEYE: bool
DOUT: bool
DPHY: bool
DREM: bool
DWRK: bool
ENG: dictionary<values=string, indices=int32>
FER: bool
GCL: bool
```

```
GCM: dictionary<values=string, indices=int32>
...
291 more columns
Use `schema()` to see entire schema
```

The output above shows that the data is divided into 884 Parquet files: 17 years' worth of data, for each of the 50 states plus Puerto Rico and the District of Columbia. After the number of columns in the dataset, we can also see the **schema**, the mapping of column names to data types. Parquet files have metadata about what each column is which is richer than text-based formats. We'll discuss types, metadata, type inference, and how you can control it, in Chapter 4.

Note that the data types are not R's data types—`numeric`, `character`, `factor`, etc.— they are from the Arrow format. As we mentioned in Chapter 1, Arrow has many more types than R, and this richer type system enables more precise control of how your data is represented. Importantly, it also allows for interoperability across systems without loss of information. These data types are similar to R data types, and some have a direct mapping to R data types, though arrow's data types also include some which don't exist in R. This interoperability is a core to the broader Arrow project. We'll get more into this in Chapter 8.

All of R's types can be represented in Arrow without loss of precision, and while there are many types in Arrow that don't have a direct mapping to types in R, nearly all have a translation that preserves the data with high fidelity. For more details, see Section A.2.2.

---

## 2.4   Querying the dataset

We have an Arrow Dataset that is pointing to multiple files on disk. Even though we can't fit the data all into memory, we can query it using dplyr-like syntax with arrow. Let's take a look at some of the questions we might want to ask about the data. For example, how did the mode of transit and average commute time change over time?

The query below is pretty complicated—but we've done that on purpose. We will talk in Chapter 3 about how we have cleaned and curated the PUMS dataset. Even with the cleaned data, we have to do a bit more processing to get this ready for analysis and plotting. First, the variable `JWTR` "Transportation to work" and `JWTRNS` "Means of transportation to work" are effectively the same content and question, but the variable measuring it was re-named starting in 2019. There were also some subtle changes to the values as well. So we start off by coalescing those two variables together and then using a `case_when` statement to align the values. We add a variable that classifies each mode into "public", "private", or "other" for ease of plotting later. Finally, we calculate the total number of commuters for each mode of transport and the mean commute durations for each. One thing to note here is that we need to calculate weighted means because of the survey methodology used [5].

---

[5]The PUMS dataset comes from surveying around 1% of the US population. It also asks a number of sensitive questions, so the Census Bureau is careful to avoid accidentally identifying specific people in the dataset. For these two reasons, the dataset is actually not the raw responses—where each row is one respondent—but rather each row has a specific weight applied to it. This weight could be thought of as something along the lines of "this number of respondents responded with this set of answers" though it is more complicated than that. Because of this, in order to make estimates about populations, we need to use the weighting columns from the dataset which tell us how many people are represented in each row to get an accurate measure in our final calculations.

Again, don't worry if this looks like a lot! We picked an example that needed some work on purpose, to show just how easily we can take the tools we know already, like dplyr, and use them with arrow on larger-than-memory datasets.

First, we'll create a couple of lists we can use in our pipeline.

```
private_transport <- c("Car, motorcycle", "Bicycle", "Walked")
public_transport <- c("Bus", "Subway, light rail", "Commuter rail, train")
```

And now we can use them in our data pipeline.

```
commute_by_mode <- pums_person |>
  mutate(
    mode_of_transit = coalesce(JWTR, JWTRNS),
    mode_of_transit = case_when(
      grepl("car|motorcycle", mode_of_transit, TRUE) ~
        "Car, motorcycle",
      grepl("bicycle", mode_of_transit, TRUE) ~ "Bicycle",
      grepl("walked", mode_of_transit, TRUE) ~ "Walked",
      grepl("bus", mode_of_transit, TRUE) ~ "Bus",
      grepl("subway|streetcar", mode_of_transit, TRUE) ~
        "Subway, light rail",
      grepl("railroad|commuter", mode_of_transit, TRUE) ~
        "Commuter rail, train",
      grepl("worked .* home", mode_of_transit, TRUE) ~
        "Worked from home",
      grepl("ferry|other", mode_of_transit, TRUE) ~
        "Other method",
      grepl("taxi", mode_of_transit, TRUE) ~ "Taxicab"
    ),
    public_private = case_when(
      mode_of_transit %in% private_transport ~ "Private",
      mode_of_transit %in% public_transport ~ "Public",
      TRUE ~ "Other"
    )
  ) |>
  filter(!is.na(mode_of_transit)) |>
  group_by(year, mode_of_transit, public_private) |>
  summarize(
    mean_commute_time = sum(JWMNP * PWGTP, na.rm = TRUE) / sum(PWGTP),
    n_commuters = sum(PWGTP)
  )

commute_by_mode |>
  collect()

# A tibble: 153 x 5
# Groups:   year, mode_of_transit [153]
    year mode_of_transit      public_private mean_commute_time
   <int> <chr>                <chr>                      <dbl>
 1  2005 Other method         Other                       34.3
 2  2005 Car, motorcycle      Private                     24.3
```

```
 3   2005 Worked from home       Other              0
 4   2005 Walked                 Private            10.6
 5   2005 Bus                    Public             43.9
 6   2005 Taxicab                Other              18.7
 7   2005 Bicycle                Private            18.1
 8   2005 Subway, light rail     Public             47.7
 9   2005 Commuter rail, train   Public             68.5
10   2006 Car, motorcycle        Private            24.2
# i 143 more rows
# i 1 more variable: n_commuters <int>
```

Now that we have our dataset containing commuters by mode of transport, we can also establish a baseline of 2005 and then calculate the percentage change for each group to make our plots relative. We do this by making a subset, `baseline`, that is just data from the year 2005 and then we use a standard join and calculate percent changes from 2005 for each year. Note, that until we call `collect()` we aren't even pulling any data into R—it's all an arrow query that we are building up.

```
baseline <- commute_by_mode |>
  filter(year == 2005) |>
  select(
    mode_of_transit,
    time_baseline = mean_commute_time,
    n_baseline = n_commuters
  )


to_plot <- commute_by_mode |>
  left_join(baseline) |>
  mutate(
    transit_type = mode_of_transit,
    mean_commute_time_relative =
      (mean_commute_time - time_baseline) / time_baseline,
    n_commuters_relative =
      (n_commuters - n_baseline) / n_baseline
  ) |>
  collect()
```

Now we can use the data in `to_plot` that we just pulled in to R to make a plot of the numbers of commuters for each mode as a change over time, as a percentage change from a 2005 baseline:

One striking thing is that we can see that after the 2020 Covid pandemic, the number of people working from home jumped to over 500% compared to 2005. There was already growth for working from home before then, but there was—understandably—a giant bump there. We also saw public transit modes drop in 2021 and then come back up in 2022.

And we can see how the commuting durations also change, as mean duration in minutes. Below we can see that, besides "Other method", all modes of transit seem to be getting longer over time, with commuter rail and bicycles seeing some of the largest increases.

As we'll see in Chapter 3, arrow has support for hundreds of functions you can call and compose this way, which allow you to do all sorts of transformations and aggregations on data that is too big to read into memory. These generally work just as they do when you

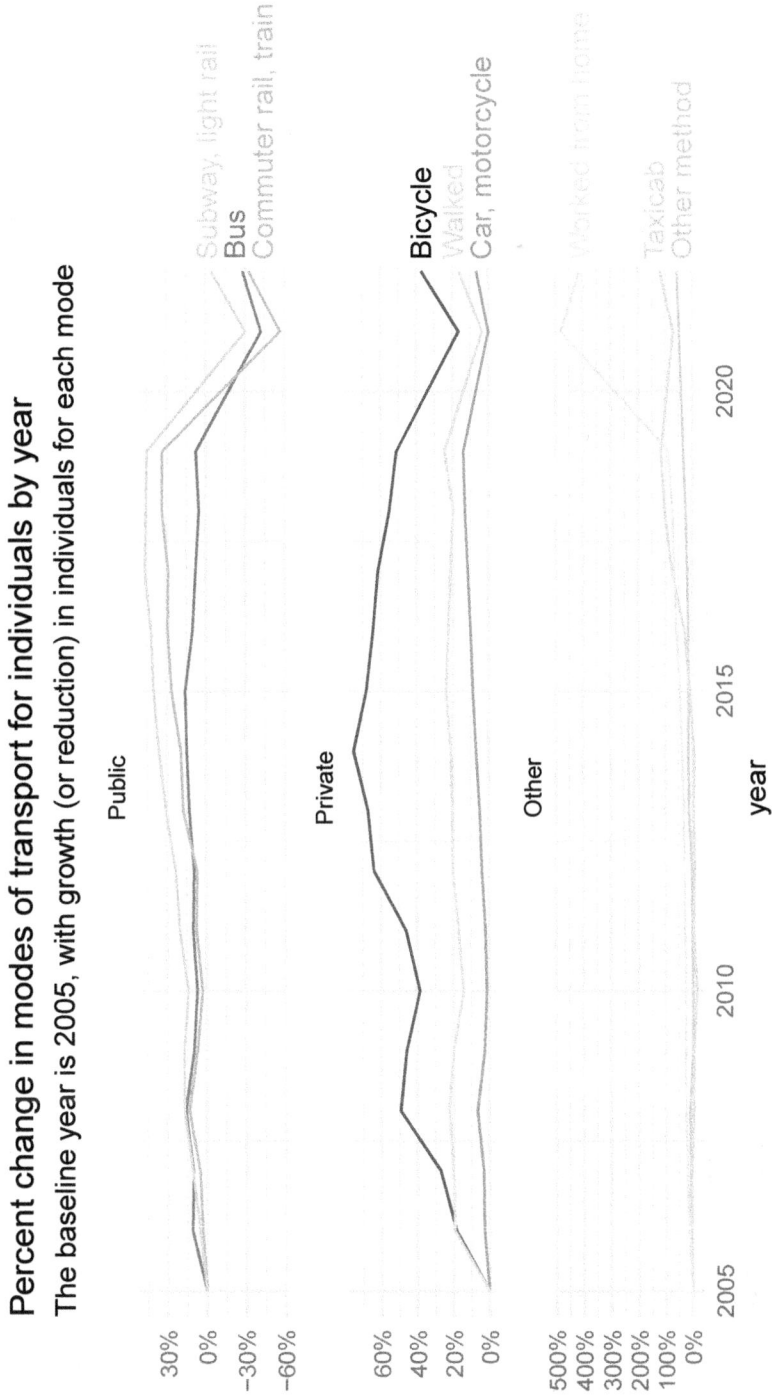

Figure 2.1: Percent change in modes of transport for individuals by year with a baseline of 2005

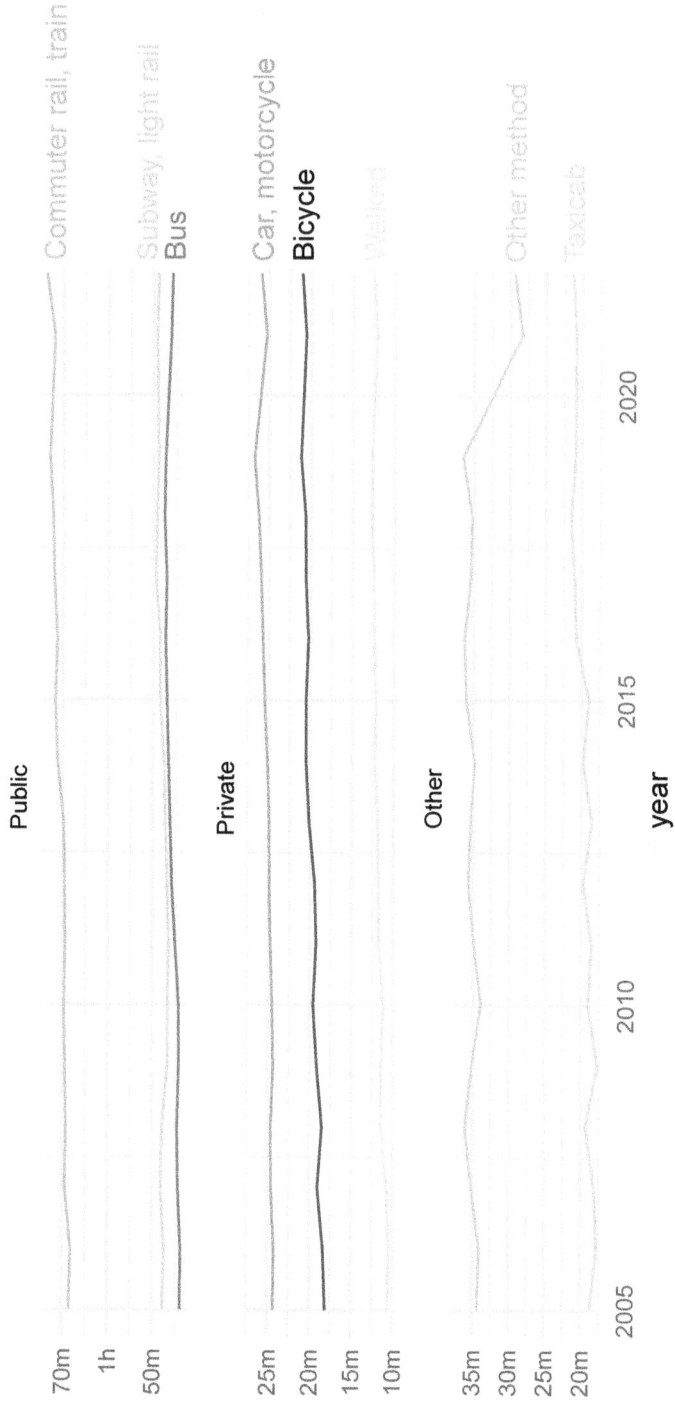

Figure 2.2: Duration of commute for different modes of transport by year

use dplyr on an in-memory R `data.frame`, with one difference: you have to call `collect()` at the end to evaluate the query. This follows the model of **dbplyr**, in which each step in the pipeline builds up a query that you then send to the database to evaluate and return the result. But with arrow, there is no remote database: everything is running in your R process.

## 2.5 How is it so easy to query such a large dataset?

Running queries like the one above so quickly on a large dataset are enabled by 3 things:

- arrow's ability to quickly process things in parallel
- the use of the Parquet format
- partitioning our data

One of the things that arrow provides is a way to read and write Parquet files in R. As we will explore in greater detail in Chapter 4, Parquet files are nice because they are fast, compressed, and store data with high fidelity. In the same way that people use "high-fidelity" to refer to audio systems which can play music without distortion or loss of quality, the same principle applies here in the context of data storage with Parquet, due to qualities of the format, such as the metadata stored alongside the data itself.

**Parquet** is a binary file format optimized for storing analytics data. Parquet files are much smaller than the equivalent CSVs, faster to work with, and also contain metadata about the schema of the data. We created a Parquet version of the PUMS dataset that we'll be using in most of the examples in this book. The Parquet version of this data is around five times smaller than a CSV version of the same data. The CSV version of the same data is around 45 GB, but the Parquet version is smaller on disk around 8.5 GB. It's even faster to query; at least 11 times for even simple queries, and sometimes much, much faster.

Earlier we mentioned that the dataset is stored in directories based on the year and location. This is called **partitioning** and Arrow is designed to take advantage of this to make dataset queries faster. It does this by only reading in the data from the partitions which are relevant to the query. For example, when we filtered the data above to only include years after 2014, Arrow only read in the data from the directories relating to 2015 onwards, and totally ignored the files from the earlier years. If you partition your data based on the variables which you query most often, this can make your queries faster. We talk more about the art and the science of partitioning datasets in Chapter 5.

## 2.6 How does this connect with the rest of the modern data ecosystem?

Now that we've introduced some of the core concepts and features of the arrow R package, we turn our attention to the ways that Arrow is structured that help you participate in a broad, modern data system. We've alluded to this a few times already how the Arrow standard was designed to be used across different technologies in the modern data stack. But let's make that concrete: what does that actually mean and why is it important?

Before the advent of standardization like the Arrow format, much—in some cases most! —of the time in data processing pipelines was spent converting data from one format to another. This process is called serialization because the data is changed into a format that is easily transported from one system to another and well known enough that each of the two systems know how to read or write it. These different formats were needed because each system generally had a specialized format it used internally and other systems didn't know how to read or interact with that or were blocked from doing so even if they could operate on it. Arrow changes this by being a modern data format that many different projects have either adopted as their internal representation or is close enough to it that they can quickly and cheaply speak arrow with other systems.

This interconnect and standardization means that it's easy to use the arrow R package alongside other packages and systems that speak Arrow, like **duckdb** and **pyarrow** (Chapter 8), or alongside geospatial packages (Section 7.5). And, because we are in the modern data world, all of this needs to be readable from cloud storage. The Arrow C++ library includes many features that let you read from cloud storage easily (Chapter 6).

# 3

## *Data Manipulation*

In the previous chapter, we took a look at an overall view of working with Arrow, but now we're going to take a closer look at how to use Arrow to efficiently transform and manipulate data using familiar dplyr syntax and approaches borrowed from the **tidyverse**. We're not going to go into too much detail about how to use dplyr in this book, but if you want to learn more or need a refresher, we recommend taking a look at the dplyr documentation[1], or R for Data Science[2].

When we introduced the PUMS dataset in the previous chapter, we saw that in its raw CSV form it takes up almost 90 GB of space on disk. As is common in data science, the raw data we start with needs some cleaning before we can do meaningful analysis.

If you want to see a walkthrough of how we cleaned the raw dataset, you can find some key examples that are useful to know about in Section 4.4, and the rest of the (somewhat repetitive) initial steps can be found in a script in this book's repository, so it doesn't distract from the task of learning about data manipulation in arrow. We include some examples of the final stages in this chapter to give you a taste of how this can be done.

In this chapter, we'll focus on data manipulation with the cleaned-up version of the data. You'll learn what approaches to take when manipulating larger-than-memory datasets, and how arrow creates queries to run against the data instead of pulling everything into the R session.

## 3.1 Building queries

We can point at all of the files and query them together as a single dataset made up of multiple Parquet files.

```
pums_person <- open_dataset("./data/person")
```

Although a lot of the cleaning has been done—we've recoded all of the character and factor variables, replaced sentinels[3] for missing values with actual missing values, etc.—there are still some data transformations that we will demonstrate using Arrow for throughout the rest of this chapter and book.

---

[1] https://dplyr.tidyverse.org

[2] https://r4ds.had.co.nz

[3] Sentinel may be an unfamiliar term—you could think of it as a placeholder value. It is used in the survey research and database worlds to refer to special values that have a special meaning. For example, you might have an age variable that can take any (positive) integer. But when the age is listed as -1 that means that the data is missing—not that someone is negative years old! This, again, is another example where old customs when CSVs and other text-based formats were the only ways to transport data forced us to do some funky things to communicate some values.

DOI: 10.1201/9781032663197-3

You can create data analysis pipelines in arrow similarly to how you would be using dplyr. For example, if you wanted to calculate the mean age of individuals from Washington across the years, you could run:[4]

```
pums_person |>
  filter(location == "wa") |>
  group_by(year) |>
  summarize(mean_age = sum(AGEP * PWGTP) / sum(PWGTP)) |>
  collect()
```

```
# A tibble: 17 x 2
    year mean_age
   <int>    <dbl>
 1  2005     36.5
 2  2009     37.1
 3  2010     37.4
 4  2013     37.9
 5  2015     38.2
 6  2016     38.4
 7  2021     39.0
 8  2006     36.7
 9  2011     37.6
10  2014     38.1
11  2012     37.8
12  2019     38.8
13  2007     36.9
14  2022     39.3
15  2008     37.2
16  2017     38.5
17  2018     38.6
```

arrow uses lazy evaluation: this means that until we call `collect()` to return the results to our R session, no data has been read into R and no calculations have been performed. Instead, we've just built a query, which describes the calculations that we want to run.

You can see this by inspecting the `pums_wa_age` object.

```
pums_wa_age <- pums_person |>
  filter(location == "wa") |>
  group_by(year) |>
  summarize(mean_age = sum(AGEP * PWGTP) / sum(PWGTP))

pums_wa_age

FileSystemDataset (query)
year: int32
```

---

[4]Note, that we might think we could use `summarize(mean_age = mean(AGEP))`, but because this dataset has row-level weights, we need to account for that in our analysis to get accurate results.

```
mean_age: double (divide(cast(..temp0, {to_type=double,
allow_int_overflow=false, allow_time_truncate=false,
allow_time_overflow=false, allow_decimal_truncate=false,
allow_float_truncate=false, allow_invalid_utf8=false}), cast(..temp1,
{to_type=double, allow_int_overflow=false, allow_time_truncate=false,
allow_time_overflow=false, allow_decimal_truncate=false,
allow_float_truncate=false, allow_invalid_utf8=false})))
```

See `$.data` for the source Arrow object

The output above shows that this object is a query on a dataset. It shows the schema of the dataset, and which columns the data is being filtered and sorted on, as well as the sort direction. At this point, no calculations have been made and won't be until we run `collect()` to execute the query and pull the results back into R.

---

## 3.2   A few more cleaning tasks

There are still a number of cleaning tasks that we should do on the dataset. With the additional processing power provided by arrow, it's possible to do these even at analysis time—which is helpful for cases where we might want to preserve the values from the underlying dataset (e.g. if we want to analyze the different wording of values over time), but when we run aggregations and queries, we want to collapse those and just run our analyses on the transformed data.

### 3.2.1   Relabeling values

It's not unusual for large datasets like PUMS, which have been collected over many years, to contain inconsistencies between how variables are reported in different partitions. One example of this is the `CIT` column, which contains data about survey respondents' US citizenship. If we compare the unique values in this column from the first year in our dataset, 2005, and a later year in the data, 2021, we can see that some of the reported labels have changed.

```
pums_person |>
  filter(year == 2005) |>
  distinct(CIT) |>
  collect()

# A tibble: 5 x 1
  CIT
  <fct>
1 Yes, born in the US
2 Yes, naturalized
3 Not a citizen
4 Yes, born abroad of American parent(s)
5 Yes, born in Puerto Rico, etc.

pums_person |>
  filter(year == 2021) |>
```

```
  distinct(CIT) |>
  collect()
```

```
# A tibble: 5 x 1
  CIT
  <fct>
1 Born in the United States
2 Not a U.S. citizen
3 U.S. citizen by naturalization
4 Born abroad of U.S. citizen parent or parents
5 Born in Puerto Rico, Guam, the U.S. Virgin Islands, or Northe~
```

In this example, despite the different labels, the values are directly analogous: the response "Yes, born in the US" in 2005 is equivalent of "Born in the United States" in 2021. If we want to use this column in an analysis, we'll need to clean it up to make sure that the values match. We can use the dplyr function `case_when()` to replace the older values with the new one, and check we've captured every possibility across the whole dataset (and not just the years 2005 and 2021) by running `distinct()` without filtering the data beforehand.

```
pums_person |>
  mutate(
    CIT = case_when(
      CIT == "Yes, born in the US" ~
        "Born in the United States",
      CIT == "Yes, naturalized" ~
        "U.S. citizen by naturalization",
      CIT == "Not a citizen" ~
        "Not a U.S. citizen",
      CIT == "Yes, born abroad of American parent(s)" ~
        "Born abroad of U.S. citizen parent or parents",
      CIT == "Yes, born in Puerto Rico, etc." ~
        paste0(
          "Born in Puerto Rico, Guam, the U.S. Virgin Islands,",
          " or Northern Marianas"
        )
    )
  ) |>
  distinct(CIT) |>
  collect()
```

```
# A tibble: 6 x 1
  CIT
  <chr>
1 Born in the United States
2 U.S. citizen by naturalization
3 Not a U.S. citizen
4 Born abroad of U.S. citizen parent or parents
5 Born in Puerto Rico, Guam, the U.S. Virgin Islands, or Northe~
6 <NA>
```

We might also want to create new columns for our analyses. For example, let's say we want to compare the relative ages of survey respondents who were self-employed versus other categories. We can use the **stringr** function `str_detect()` to create a new column, which contains TRUE if the string "Self-employed" is present in the COW (category of work) columns and FALSE if it is now.

```
library(stringr)

pums_person |>
  mutate(COW = as.character(COW)) |>
  mutate(self_employed = str_detect(COW, "Self-employed")) |>
  group_by(year, self_employed) |>
  summarize(mean_age = sum(AGEP * PWGTP) / sum(PWGTP)) |>
  arrange(year, self_employed) |>
  collect()
```

```
# A tibble: 51 x 3
# Groups:   year [17]
    year self_employed mean_age
   <int> <lgl>            <dbl>
 1  2005 FALSE             40.2
 2  2005 TRUE              47.8
 3  2005 NA                29.3
 4  2006 FALSE             39.9
 5  2006 TRUE              47.8
 6  2006 NA                30.5
 7  2007 FALSE             40.1
 8  2007 TRUE              48.1
 9  2007 NA                30.6
10  2008 FALSE             40.4
# i 41 more rows
```

Now we've seen that we can work with familiar dplyr and tidyverse syntax on this large dataset using arrow, we're going to talk more about exactly how this works.

## 3.3   Workflows for larger datasets

Why does arrow avoid computing on the data until you explicitly tell it to? While you can work with Arrow data in memory, the biggest benefits of arrow come from its ability to work with data that is too big to fit into memory. After all, if the data were small enough to fit into memory, you would have many more tools available to you, both in R itself and in other packages. Since arrow is designed to work with larger-than-memory datasets, and calculations on such large data may be slow to complete, you should be clear about when you want to run such a query. The package doesn't want to surprise you by crashing your session by running out of memory.

If the output of your query is larger-than-memory, you won't be able to return it to your R session without crashing it, and so this may require a different approach to validating your results.

Let's say you want to create a new query which looks at whether individuals over the age of 18 in the data have spent time in higher education or not. You might start off with something like this:

```
higher_ed_string <- "(Bach|Mast|Prof|Doct|college|degree)"
higher_ed <- pums_person |>
  filter(AGEP > 18) |>
  mutate(higher_education = grepl(higher_ed_string, SCHL))
```

You can preview your results using **head()** to only return the first few rows, and calling **select()** will speed things up further, as arrow will only read into memory the requested columns.

```
head(higher_ed, 20) |>
  select(SCHL, higher_education) |>
  collect()
```

```
# A tibble: 20 x 2
   SCHL                              higher_education
   <chr>                             <lgl>
 1 Bachelor's degree                 TRUE
 2 Doctorate degree                  TRUE
 3 High school graduate              FALSE
 4 11th Grade                        FALSE
 5 Associate degree                  TRUE
 6 1+ years of college, no degree    TRUE
 7 Bachelor's degree                 TRUE
 8 1+ years of college, no degree    TRUE
 9 Master's degree                   TRUE
10 1+ years of college, no degree    TRUE
11 1+ years of college, no degree    TRUE
12 High school graduate              FALSE
13 Bachelor's degree                 TRUE
14 Bachelor's degree                 TRUE
15 Associate degree                  TRUE
16 1+ years of college, no degree    TRUE
17 High school graduate              FALSE
18 Some college, but less than 1 year TRUE
19 Associate degree                  TRUE
20 High school graduate              FALSE
```

Alternatively, if you want a preview of the dataset which contains the number of rows to be returned from your query, as well as preserving the original Arrow data types, you can call **glimpse()** to show this information.

```
higher_ed |>
  select(SCHL, higher_education) |>
  glimpse()
```

```
FileSystemDataset with 884 Parquet files (query)
41,254,553 rows x 2 columns
$ SCHL             <string> "Bachelor's degree", "Doctorate degree~
$ higher_education <bool> TRUE, TRUE, FALSE, FALSE, TRUE, TRUE, ~
Call `print()` for query details
```

## 3.4  Using functions inside dplyr pipelines

A number of dplyr functions allow you to embed other functions in them. `mutate()` is a prime example of this, where we are changing some data in the data frame using other functions from base R or other packages. Many tidyverse functions will simply work out of the box with arrow queries. For example, as arrow has code that works just like the stringr function `str_detect()`—which works out if a string is present in a column or not—we can use it in an arrow dplyr pipeline just like we would a standard dplyr pipeline. For more details about how this works, see Section 3.6 below.

```
higher_ed <- pums_person |>
  filter(AGEP > 18) |>
  mutate(higher_education = stringr::str_detect(
    SCHL,
    higher_ed_string)
  )
```

You can use these functions with or without namespacing, so either `stringr::str_detect()` or just `str_detect()` work.

When we wrote this book, there were 37 dplyr functions and 211 other functions available in arrow—though this number may have increased since! We've demonstrated some string operations here; both the base R and stringr flavors are supported. There is also deep support for **lubridate** functions for working with date and time data.[5] If you want to find out which functions are available in arrow, you can view the help page which lists all of the dplyr functions and other function mappings by calling `?acero`.

While many functions are implemented in arrow, you aren't limited by just what is included in the package. Sometimes it is convenient or necessary to write your own functions. For example, you might need to convert the `JWMNP` (commute time) columns from minutes to hours and have written a function which does this conversion for you. What happens if you then try to run this function in arrow?

```
time_hours_rounded <- function(mins){
  round(mins/60, 2)
}

pums_person |>
  select(JWMNP) |>
  mutate(commute_hours = time_hours_rounded(JWMNP)) |>
  head() |>
  collect()

# A tibble: 6 x 2
  JWMNP commute_hours
```

---

[5]The 2022 UseR! conference workshop on arrow, "Larger-Than-Memory Data Workflows with Apache Arrow," by Danielle Navarro, Jonathan Keane, and Stephanie Hazlitt, has some good examples that show more functions being used, including datetime functions. See https://arrow-user2022.netlify.app/. We figured everyone had seen enough of the NYC taxi dataset and chose to use U.S. Census data for examples in this book. This means we can show some more interesting queries and results, but unfortunately, there is no interesting datetime data in it!

```
        <int>         <dbl>
1         5           0.08
2        15           0.25
3        NA           NA
4        NA           NA
5        NA           NA
6        50           0.83
```

Great, this has worked! Arrow is able to look at the body of the `time_hours_rounded()` function and map the code there to the equivalent code which can be run by Acero.

Let's now take a look at an example which doesn't work as easily. The `SOCP` column in the dataset contains Standard Occupational Classification (SOC) codes, which are in capital letters.

```
pums_person |>
  select(SOCP) |>
  distinct() |>
  head() |>
  collect()
```

```
# A tibble: 6 x 1
  SOCP
  <chr>
1 MGR-PROPERTY, REAL ESTATE, AND COMMUNITY ASSOCIATION MANAGERS
2 EDU-POSTSECONDARY TEACHERS
3 <NA>
4 UNEMPLOYED, WITH NO WORK EXPERIENCE IN THE LAST 5 YEARS**
5 EAT-DISHWASHERS
6 MED-REGISTERED NURSES
```

If we wanted to convert these into sentence case, with just the first letter of each sentence capitalized, we might look at using the helpful function `str_to_sentence()` from stringr. However, if we call this, we get an error.

```
pums_person |>
  select(SOCP) |>
  mutate(SOCP = stringr::str_to_sentence(SOCP)) |>
  distinct() |>
  head() |>
  collect()
```

```
Error in `stringr::str_to_sentence()`:
! Expression not supported in Arrow
> Call collect() first to pull data into R.
```

The error message shows that this expression is not supported in Arrow. This is because there is no Arrow C++ function that is the equivalent of `stringr::str_to_sentence()` and so it is not supported in the arrow R package. So what should you do if you encounter this?

If the resulting data in your pipeline is small enough, you could pull the data back into R, and then continue your analysis. This isn't always an option though, so what should you do if your data is still too large to return to R memory? Find out more about this in a few sections when we talk about user-defined functions (Section 7.3).

## 3.5  Joins

**Joins** are used to combine data from 2 or more sources, based on columns that these sources have in common. The columns that we want to use to match our data sources are sometimes referred to as **join keys**.

Let's say for example, we want to compare the commute time of each person in the dataset to the (weighted) mean commute time for their state. We could express this more concisely using `mutate()`, like this:

```
pums_person |>
  group_by(location, year) |>
  mutate(
    commute_diff = JWMNP - sum(JWMNP * PWGTP, na.rm = TRUE) /
      sum(PWGTP)
  )
```

But, to illustrate some properties of joins, we'll decompose that into a calculation of a mean value, which we'll then join back onto the main dataset.

We start by creating a reference table of mean commute time by state and year.

```
mean_commute_time <- pums_person |>
  group_by(location, year) |>
  summarize(
    mean_commute_time = sum(JWMNP * PWGTP, na.rm = TRUE) / sum(PWGTP)
  ) |>
  collect()

head(mean_commute_time, 5)
```

```
# A tibble: 5 x 3
# Groups:   location [5]
  location  year mean_commute_time
  <chr>    <int>             <dbl>
1 al        2005              9.96
2 ca        2005             11.4
3 fl        2005             11.1
4 mi        2005             10.2
5 nh        2005             12.7
```

We can then perform a left join to combine this information with the information in the original datasets.

The code to accomplish this looks something like this:

```
pums_person |>
  left_join(mean_commute_time, by = c("location", "year")) |>
  mutate(commute_diff = JWMNP - mean_commute_time) |>
  select(
    commute_diff,
    commute_time = JWMNP,
```

x

| year | location | SERIALNO | JWMNP |
|------|----------|----------|-------|
| 2005 | ny | 177 | 5 |
| 2005 | ca | 1404 | 15 |
| 2005 | ny | 2378 | 50 |
| 2006 | ny | 2876 | NA |
| 2006 | ny | 1129 | 25 |
| 2006 | ca | 2764 | 10 |
| 2006 | ca | 1799 | 40 |
| 2007 | ny | 2146 | 35 |
| 2007 | ny | 357 | 15 |
| ... | ... | ... | ... |

y

| year | location | mean_commute_time |
|------|----------|-------------------|
| 2005 | ny | 12.43 |
| 2006 | ny | 13.83 |
| 2007 | ny | 12.09 |
| 2005 | ca | 11.38 |
| 2006 | ca | 12.15 |
| ... | ... | ... |

left_join(x, y, by = c("year", "location"))

| year | location | SERIALNO | JWMNP | mean_commute_time |
|------|----------|----------|-------|-------------------|
| 2005 | ny | 177 | 5 | 12.43 |
| 2005 | ca | 1404 | 15 | 11.38 |
| 2005 | ny | 2378 | 50 | 12.43 |
| 2006 | ny | 2876 | NA | 13.83 |
| 2006 | ny | 1129 | 25 | 13.83 |
| 2006 | ca | 2764 | 10 | 12.15 |
| 2006 | ca | 1799 | 40 | 12.15 |
| 2007 | ny | 2146 | 35 | 12.09 |
| 2007 | ny | 357 | 15 | 12.09 |
| ... | ... | ... | ... | ... |

Figure 3.1: Example tables for joining data

```
  mean_commute_time
) |>
head(3) |>
collect()
```

```
# A tibble: 3 x 3
  commute_diff commute_time mean_commute_time
         <dbl>        <int>             <dbl>
1        -3.18            5              8.18
2         6.82           15              8.18
3        NA             NA               8.18
```

### 3.5.1 Join keys

One important thing to know about doing joins in arrow is that the data types of the join key columns must match. Let's say we decided that we want to change the data type of the year column from a 32-bit integer to an 16-bit integer. We can change the column type using cast(), but if we then try to join our reference table, we get an error.

```
pums_person |>
  mutate(year = cast(year, int16())) |>
  left_join(mean_commute_time, by = c("location", "year"))|>
  head() |>
  collect()
```

```
Error in `compute.arrow_dplyr_query()`:
! Invalid: Incompatible data types for corresponding join field keys:
FieldRef.Name(year) of type int16 and FieldRef.Name(year) of type int32
```

The source of the error is in the difference in data types for the **year** column: we updated it in the main dataset to be an **int16()**, but in the reference table, the **year** column is still an **int32()**. We can verify this by using the **schema()** function.

```
schema(mean_commute_time)
```

```
Schema
location: string
year: int32
mean_commute_time: double
```

To be able to perform the join, we must update one or both of the datasets so that the types match. The simplest thing to do in our case is update the data type of the lookup table.

In this example, we called **collect()** to pull our **mean_commute_time** reference table into our R session, and so it is a tibble. When we perform joins to data.frame or tibble object (we'll just call these "data frames" from here on), arrow converts this object into an **Arrow Table**.

An Arrow Table is equivalent to an R data frame. The key difference here is that the columns types are Arrow data types instead of R data types. When an Arrow Table is created from an R data frame, the data type of each column is automatically converted into its Arrow equivalent. For the most part, this automatic conversion is fine to ignore, but in some circumstances, like joining tables, we might want to manually specify the data types to convert to instead.

We can manually set the schema of the reference table by converting it to an Arrow Table ourselves and setting the schema at the same time.

```
mean_commute_time_arrow <- arrow_table(
  mean_commute_time,
  schema = schema(
    location = string(),
    year = int16(),
    mean_commute_time = double()
  )
)
```

```
schema(mean_commute_time_arrow)
```

```
Schema
location: string
year: int16
mean_commute_time: double
```

```
See $metadata for additional Schema metadata
```

The data type of the join key in the reference table now matches the data type in our original dataset, and now the join will work.

```
pums_person |>
 mutate(year = cast(year, int16())) |>
 left_join(
   mean_commute_time_arrow,
   by = c("location", "year")
 )|>
 mutate(commute_diff = mean_commute_time - JWMNP) |>
 select(
   commute_diff,
   commute_time = JWMNP,
   mean_commute_time
 ) |>
 head(3) |>
 collect()
```

```
# A tibble: 3 x 3
  commute_diff commute_time mean_commute_time
         <dbl>        <int>             <dbl>
1           NA            5                NA
2           NA           15                NA
3           NA           NA                NA
```

Joins are not restricted to data frames or Arrow Tables. You can join across datasets and across queries on datasets.

We could have instead defined the query for `mean_compute_time` and not called `collect()`, and we could use that in the join.

```
mean_commute_time <- pums_person |>
  group_by(location, year) |>
  summarize(
    mean_commute_time = sum(JWMNP * PWGTP, na.rm = TRUE) /
      sum(PWGTP)
  )
```

```
pums_person |>
  left_join(mean_commute_time, by = c("location", "year")) |>
  mutate(commute_diff = JWMNP - mean_commute_time)
```

We'll take a closer look at joins again in Section 4.4 in a practical example where we explore combining a dataset with a reference table. Section 7.5.5 also shows a practical use case of several kinds of joins to prepare sparse data for plotting. If you're interested in other methods of combining data from different sources, check out Section 5.7.3 where we show an example of querying data in different formats as a single dataset.

## 3.6  How does all of this work? Verbs, functions, and arrow objects

The arrow R package contains a **dplyr backend**, an implementation of dplyr methods and functions that allows you to work with data using the same dplyr functionality you may be accustomed to using with regular R data frames.

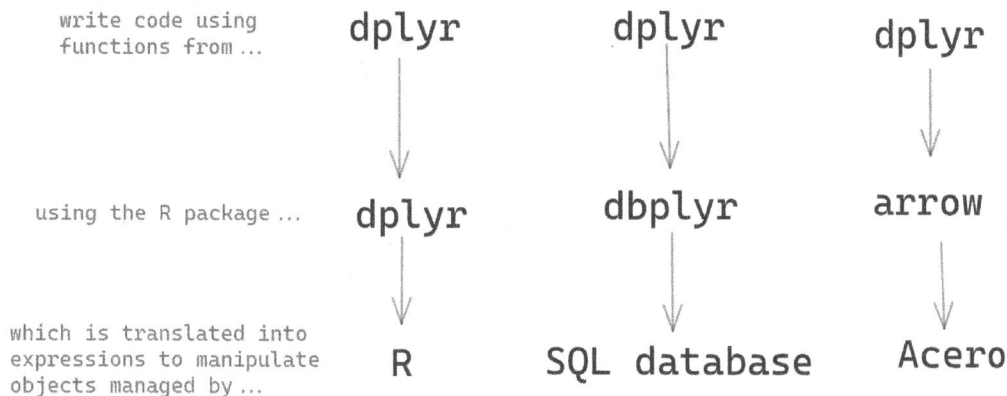

Figure 3.2: How the arrow R package works

How can you write dplyr code that looks like what you'd use when exploring an in-memory data frame and have it automatically be translated to run on a larger-than-memory arrow Dataset? The arrow R package makes use of two defining features of R: S3 methods and non-standard evaluation.

We refer to the various functions in dplyr that operate on one or more data frames—things like `select()`, `filter()`, `summarize()`—as **verbs**, as they all do actions to the data. In dplyr, these are implemented as **generics**, which means that they are open to extension by other packages. The dbplyr package, for example, defines methods for `select()` and the other verbs that operate on different databases. In arrow, there are methods defined for arrow Datasets and Tables, so that when you call `dplyr::select(Dataset, ...)`, the version of `select()` that is defined for `arrow::Dataset` is called.

Most functions in R are not generics, however, so arrow can't solve everything by implementing methods. Instead, inside the arrow methods for dplyr verbs, the arguments you provide are evaluated in a special environment that contains alternative versions of many base R and tidyverse functions. These alternatives don't immediately execute and return the result; instead, they return arrow **Expressions**, which capture the intent of your code and express it in a way that can be understood by Acero, the Arrow query engine. This is similar to how dbplyr turns your R code into SQL.

We refer to these alternative versions of R functions that return Expressions as **bindings**. The arrow R package contains bindings for hundreds of functions, many from base R packages, as well as from tidyverse packages, notably lubridate, stringr, and tidyselect. For a full list of what dplyr verbs and functions have arrow bindings, see `?acero` in the package.

## 3.7  Conclusion

In this chapter we covered manipulating data with data that is larger than memory by using Arrow Datasets. This allowed us to run analyses on datasets that in total are larger than can fit into memory but between clever partitioning and some parts of the way that Arrow executes queries, we can efficiently manipulate this data without needing to get a larger computer or write the piece-meal processing code ourselves. The next chapter will go into more details about how and why datasets work in Arrow for a deeper understanding of the capabilities, caveats, and best practices.

# 4

# *Files and Formats*

In the previous chapter, we started exploring a dataset made up of CSV files, and then skipped ahead to working with a version we'd converted to Parquet files. While CSVs are ubiquitous, Parquet files have a lot of nice features that make them ideal for analytic workloads:

- they can preserve rich type information
- they're smaller on disk
- they're faster to read in

In this chapter, we'll explore the different file formats that Arrow can read and write, focusing particularly on the tools you need to ingest data from CSVs and store them in Parquet files with high fidelity.

We'll start off by creating a directory to work with temporary files created in this chapter.

```
tmp_dir <- "./data/transient_data"
dir.create(tmp_dir)
```

## 4.1 Overview of supported formats

Arrow supports reading and writing files in multiple formats:

- CSV and other text-delimited formats
- newline-delimited JSON
- Parquet
- the Arrow format itself

The functions for reading and writing individual files in arrow are shown in Table 4.1.

Table 4.1: Functions for reading and writing individual files

| Format | Reading | Writing |
|---|---|---|
| CSV or other delimited file | read_delim_arrow() <br> read_csv_arrow() <br> read_csv2_arrow() <br> read_tsv_arrow() | write_csv_arrow() |
| Newline-delimited JSON | read_json_arrow() | (Not supported) |
| Parquet | read_parquet() | write_parquet() |
| Arrow IPC Format (formerly Feather) | read_ipc_file() <br> read_feather() | write_ipc_file() <br> write_feather() |

DOI: 10.1201/9781032663197-4

Let's briefly review the file formats.

### 4.1.1  CSV

A **CSV** is one of the simplest and most widely-known formats for data storage and sharing. It is a plain-text file in which each line is a row of data, and values are separated into columns by commas (hence "comma-separated values"). CSV is the most common of a family of text-delimited formats; any character can be used as a delimiter, such as `tab` (as in TSV) or semicolon.

The CSV's main strength is that everyone and everything can read it. However, CSVs have some serious limitations. Most importantly, CSVs do not contain all of the information you need to read in the data faithfully. Because the data is encoded as text, and because there is no standard way to indicate what the data types are for each column, you either have to specify types yourself, or allow the library to attempt to guess the types. Essentially, CSVs are a lossy file format: when you write out data to a CSV and read it back in, features of the data are lost because they are not contained in the file.

The encoding of data as text has other costs as well. Because you have to parse strings to read numbers, and have to convert numbers to strings when writing, there's a *serialization* cost relative to binary formats that can represent these types natively. Text is also inefficient for representing numbers: for example, the number `-2147483647` takes up 88 bits as text (11 characters, 8 bits each), but if stored in its numeric form can be represented a 32-bit integer.

### 4.1.2  Newline-delimited JSON

Another format supported by Arrow is newline-delimited JSON (**NDJSON**), also known as JSON lines (JSONL). This format is a subset of JSON, and is different from other JSON formats in that each line is a JSON object with a shared schema. It is commonly used for streaming data.

NDJSON files look something like this:

```
{"species": "cat", "sounds": ["meow", "purr", "hiss"]}
{"species": "dog", "sounds": ["woof", "bark", "growl"]}
{"species": "bird", "sounds": ["tweet", "squawk"]}
```

One advantage of NDJSON is that it is both human-readable and supports nested data structures. JSON also has a slightly richer type system than CSV. For example, `true` is parsed as a boolean value and not a string. However, it only supports primitive types (string, number, boolean, object) and is still a text-based format, so it requires parsing and is large on disk, typically larger than a comparable CSV because the column names are repeated in each row.

```
writeLines(
  c(
    '{"species": "cat", "sounds": ["meow", "purr", "hiss"]}',
    '{"species": "dog", "sounds": ["woof", "bark", "growl"]}',
    '{"species": "bird", "sounds": ["tweet", "squawk"]}'
  ),
  file.path(tmp_dir, "animals.jsonl")
)
```

```
read_json_arrow(file.path(tmp_dir, "animals.jsonl"))
```

```
# A tibble: 3 x 2
  species            sounds
  <chr>     <list<character>>
1 cat                    [3]
2 dog                    [3]
3 bird                   [2]
```

Arrow supports reading NDJSON files, but at the time of writing does not support writing them.

### 4.1.3 Parquet

**Parquet**[1] is a standard, open format widely used in the big data ecosystem. It is a binary file format: Parquet files are designed to be read by computers rather than humans. This means that unlike CSVs, you can't just open them in a text editor and inspect the contents. It is also a columnar format, meaning that data in each column is saved together, as opposed to CSVs and many other text-based formats, which are row based.

Parquet files have a number of features that make them small on disk, fast to read in, and optimal for analytic workloads. They support many compression algorithms and data encodings, and they can include statistics about the data in them that systems can take advantage of to speed up reading and querying data even further. We generally recommend using Parquet files unless there is a compelling reason not to.

### 4.1.4 Arrow and Feather

**Feather**[2] was originally developed as a prototype by Hadley Wickham and Wes McKinney to implement the Arrow format, and demonstrate rapid sharing of data between R and Python. It was not exactly "Arrow" as it did not support all data types, but it did demonstrate the value of having a common data format that could be read across languages efficiently and with high fidelity.

The Arrow inter-process-communication (**IPC**) format—that is, the bits in memory—can also be written to disk. (At one point, this bore the "Feather V2" label, but that has since been dropped.) There are some circumstances where this is useful. Because the uncompressed[3] data is exactly the same as what is in memory, there is zero serialization cost to accessing it, and you can memory-map the file, allowing the software to read in chunks of it lazily.

That said, the Arrow developer community generally does not recommend storing data in Arrow IPC format on disk.[4] For most applications, Parquet is a better choice for storage. Parquet files tend to be smaller on disk, which means faster to transfer over the network, and despite having to decompress and decode, can still be faster to read into memory, because less memory needs to be moved around. They're also widely supported across many data

---

[1]https://parquet.apache.org/

[2]https://posit.co/blog/feather/

[3]The Arrow IPC file format also supports compression, though if you use it, it's no longer the case that there's no serialization, and you can't memory-map it.

[4]https://arrow.apache.org/faq/

systems.

---

💡 Arrow? Feather? IPC? Parquet?

We frequently get questions and see confusion about these different formats. Given the history we talk about above, it's not totally surprising that Arrow, Feather, and IPC aren't totally clear. So here are short summaries of each:

**Arrow IPC**: the Arrow in-memory format and layout, written to disk.

**Feather**: Version 1 was a precursor to Arrow and is now deprecated. It is very close to the Arrow format, though doesn't have all of the types. Version 2 is the same thing as Arrow IPC, though that name has fallen out of favor.

**Parquet**: A standard, open, modern, column-oriented data storage format.

"Feather" as a name will see less and less use since Version 1 is deprecated and the Arrow community has started using the name "Arrow IPC" instead.

Like we recommend in this chapter: if you're looking for a format to store data in today, pick Parquet unless you have good and specific technical reasons for needing Arrow IPC.

---

### 4.1.5 Summary

Table 4.2 summarizes the features and tradeoffs of the file formats that arrow works with.

Table 4.2: Comparison of formats supported by Arrow

|                                 | CSV | ND-JSON | Parquet | Arrow |
|---------------------------------|-----|---------|---------|-------|
| Read using Arrow                | x   | x       | x       | x     |
| Write using Arrow               | x   |         | x       | x     |
| Human-readable                  | x   | x       |         |       |
| Fast read/write                 |     |         | x       | x     |
| Includes schema                 |     |         | x       | x     |
| Metadata                        |     |         | x       | x     |
| Nested structures               |     | x       | x       | x     |
| Compression                     |     |         | x       | x     |
| High-fidelity type preservation |     |         | x       | x     |
| Widely adopted                  | x   |         | x       |       |

Now that we've surveyed the file formats, we're going to discuss how to read in CSVs effectively since they are both widespread and potentially challenging. We'll also demonstrate why exactly Parquet files are beneficial in terms of file size, speed, and fidelity, and show you how to convert your CSV data into Parquet files.

---

## 4.2   Reading CSVs

Let's explore the tools the arrow R package provides to help us work with CSVs. Because they don't contain all of the information you need to understand the data, and they can vary greatly in structure, we'll need to get familiar with the range of options you can provide to the reader functions. We're going to be looking at a subset of the PUMS dataset, which contains fewer columns than the full dataset.

### 4.2.1 The basics

The functions in arrow for reading delimited file formats are:

- `read_csv_arrow()`
- `read_csv2_arrow()` (for semicolon-delimited data)
- `read_tsv_arrow()` (tab-delimited)
- `read_delim_arrow()`, the general-purpose function

If you've used the **readr** package, you should find these familiar to use, as many of the argument names match those in **readr::read_delim()** For example, if you want to specify that the string "none" represents an NA value, and to only read in particular columns of the data, you can use the **na** and **col_select** arguments.

```
read_csv_arrow(
  "./data/raw_csvs/person/2021/ak/psam_p02.csv",
  na = "none",
  col_select = c("AGEP", "SCHL")
)
```

See the docs for `?read_csv_arrow()` for the full list of options supported.

When you use one of these functions to read a file, it will be read in as an **Arrow Table**, the Arrow equivalent of a data frame, and then converted to a tibble automatically. If instead you want the data to remain as an Arrow Table, you should set the **as_data_frame** argument to FALSE.

```
# Read in the CSV as an Arrow Table
read_csv_arrow(
  "./data/raw_csvs/person/2021/ak/psam_p02.csv",
  as_data_frame = FALSE
)
```

You can do all of the same dplyr operations on Tables as you can on Datasets. The difference is that with Tables, the data is already in memory.

In this book, we're focusing on examples using Datasets because if your data can already fit into memory, you have many options for how to analyze your data. Arrow is great, but if you are just trying to analyze data that fits into memory, it's probably unnecessary.

That said, there are some cases where it is useful to read a file in as a Table. We'll highlight a few of them below.

### 4.2.2 Type inference and schemas

Because CSVs do not contain information about the types of the columns of data in them, when reading one in, you either specify the types explicitly, as in the **col_types** argument to the readr functions, or you let the CSV reader try to infer the types by inspecting the first chunk of data. Often, the type inference is just fine.

Sometimes, however, it can be wildly wrong. When arrow is working out the schema of a column, it guesses the simplest possible type that can describe all the values. The problem with relying on schema inference like this is that if you have a dataset where the first few rows of data are not representative of the rest of the dataset, you may end up with an incorrect schema.

For example, if arrow sees the values 1, 2, and 3, it might guess that these are integer values, but if arrow sees the values 1, 2, and 3.1, then arrow will see that column cannot be integers and must be made of doubles. You can see how this could cause an inference problem: if the reader infers that a column is integers, but then decimal value appear later, they won't be read correctly.

Another problem is that even if the data is representative, the guess might be wrong. Classic examples of this are things like phone numbers or US zip codes. They are made up entirely of numbers, but schema inference may treat them as integers and strip the leading 0, instead of the correct approach of treating them as strings, and so, when you try to read in the dataset later, you may get an error or incorrect results.

In our dataset, the `PUMA` variable (short for Public Use Microdata Area) represents micro-level geographic areas. They are similar to US zip codes: they are a 5-digit number that may include a leading zero.

You can see here on the first few rows, the `PUMA` values are `"00101"`, `"00101"`, `"00102"`, and `"00200"`.

```
readLines("./data/raw_csvs/person/2021/ak/psam_p02.csv", n = 5)
```

```
[1] "RT,SERIALNO,DIVISION,SPORDER,PUMA,REGION,ST,ADJINC,PWGTP,AGEP,CIT,C...
[2] "P,2021GQ0000239,9,01,00101,4,02,1029928,38,21,1,,5,2,2,2,2,2,,2,2,,...
[3] "P,2021GQ0000288,9,01,00101,4,02,1029928,151,21,1,,5,2,2,2,2,1,,2,2,...
[4] "P,2021GQ0000315,9,01,00102,4,02,1029928,69,91,1,,,1,2,1,1,1,,2,1,1,...
[5] "P,2021GQ0000499,9,01,00200,4,02,1029928,16,30,1,,5,2,2,2,2,2,,,2,,,...
```

However, if we read in our CSV subset without providing a schema, despite the leading zeroes being present in the data, the data type of this column is inferred to be an integer.

```
pums_csv_one_state <- read_csv_arrow(
  "./data/raw_csvs/person/2021/ak/psam_p02.csv"
)


head(schema(pums_csv_one_state))


Schema
RT: string
SERIALNO: string
DIVISION: int32
SPORDER: int32
PUMA: int32
REGION: int32
```

This is incorrect, and could cause us problems later, for instance, if we wanted to use this column to join to another dataset which correctly records `PUMA` as a string. If we were to convert this to a string, we'd have to make sure that any values were correctly padded with leading zeroes—that is, we would have to convert the integer `101` to string `"00101"`. This is also extra unnecessary processing: the original data is already string and we'd be converting from string to integer and then back to string again.

Instead of doing this though, we can specify the data types before we read in the data, using the `schema` argument.

```
# Read CSV file and specify a schema
read_csv_arrow(
  "./data/raw_csvs/person/2021/ak/psam_p02.csv",
  schema = schema(
    location = string(),
    year = int32(),
    AGEP = int32(),
    SCHL = string(),
    PUMA = string(),
    JWMNP = int32(),
    JWTR = string(),
    WKWN = int32(),
    HICOV = bool(),
    WRK = bool()
  ),
  skip = 1
)
```

Note that we also added `skip = 1`. As with other CSV readers, if the file contains a header row with column names, but you provide them yourself, you need to tell the reader to skip the header row rather than try to read it in as data. By providing the `schema`, we're defining both the names and types, so we likewise need to tell the reader to skip the first row.

Another thing to note is that we have specified the `int32` type for the integers. If you want control of the precision of the integers or floating-point numbers, you can't rely on the type inference because it only chooses the largest size: `int64` and `float64`. If you know the range of integer values in the data is small, for example, and you wanted to save on memory, you would want to be able to specify a smaller type, like `int8`. Or as we have done here, if you expected to pull a large amount of data into R, you might want `int32` because integers in R are 32-bit. This is not required—unlike with the `PUMA` variable, the integers will be parsed correctly, but they will just require more memory than they need and will require a small amount of translation to step down from `int64` to `int32`. Sometimes, that savings will be meaningful.

But what if you're working with a file with a lot of columns—do you really have to type this all out by hand? Absolutely not!

One option is to supply column types for a subset of columns, by providing a partial schema using the `col_types` argument.

```
# Read CSV file and specify a partial schema
read_csv_arrow(
  "./data/raw_csvs/person/2021/ak/psam_p02.csv",
  col_types = schema(PUMA = string())
)
```

Because we only supplied a partial schema, Arrow still needs to read the headers of the other columns and infer their types, and so in this case we don't need to pass in `skip = 1` like we did when we passed in the full schema.

Another option is to take the schema which is inferred by arrow and manually update it yourself before reading in the file again. You can extract the schema using the `schema()` function.

```
# Read in the file as an Arrow Table and get its schema
pums_csv_one_state <- read_csv_arrow(
  "./data/raw_csvs/person/2021/ak/psam_p02.csv"
)

one_state_schema <- schema(pums_csv_one_state)
```

Schemas can be interacted with like lists in R, and so if we want to look more closely at one of these column name to data type mappings, we can extract it using the [[ or $ operator.

```
one_state_schema[["PUMA"]]
```

```
Field
PUMA: int32
```

We can also assign in different types, and then provide the modified schema when re-reading the file to use those types.

```
# Update the data types of the PUMA field
one_state_schema[["PUMA"]] <- string()
```

```
# Read in the file, using the updated schema
read_csv_arrow(
  "./data/raw_csvs/person/2021/ak/psam_p02.csv",
  schema = one_state_schema,
  skip = 1
)
```

```
# A tibble: 6,411 x 287
      RT    SERIALNO   DIVISION SPORDER PUMA  REGION    ST ADJINC
      <chr> <chr>         <int>   <int> <chr>  <int> <int>  <int>
  1 P     2021GQ00002~        9       1 00101      4     2 1.03e6
  2 P     2021GQ00002~        9       1 00101      4     2 1.03e6
  3 P     2021GQ00003~        9       1 00102      4     2 1.03e6
  4 P     2021GQ00004~        9       1 00200      4     2 1.03e6
  5 P     2021GQ00011~        9       1 00400      4     2 1.03e6
  6 P     2021GQ00016~        9       1 00101      4     2 1.03e6
  7 P     2021GQ00018~        9       1 00300      4     2 1.03e6
  8 P     2021GQ00019~        9       1 00300      4     2 1.03e6
  9 P     2021GQ00020~        9       1 00400      4     2 1.03e6
 10 P     2021GQ00021~        9       1 00101      4     2 1.03e6
# i 6,401 more rows
# i 279 more variables: PWGTP <int>, AGEP <int>, CIT <int>,
#   CITWP <int>, COW <int>, DDRS <int>, DEAR <int>, DEYE <int>,
#   DOUT <int>, DPHY <int>, DRAT <int>, DRATX <int>,
#   DREM <int>, ENG <int>, FER <int>, GCL <int>, GCM <int>,
#   GCR <int>, HIMRKS <int>, HINS1 <int>, HINS2 <int>,
#   HINS3 <int>, HINS4 <int>, HINS5 <int>, HINS6 <int>, ...
```

What if you want to save the schema in a script, instead of loading it and updating it all the time? You can use the `code()` method to extract the code from the schema, which you can then copy and paste into your script. We subset the schema with [c("RT", "SERIALNO",

"DIVISION", "SPORDER", "PUMA", "REGION", "ST")] only for clarity and space savings in the book. In real use, call **one_state_schema$code()** to use the whole schema.

```
# Print the code needed to create this schema
subset_cols <- c("RT", "SERIALNO", "DIVISION", "SPORDER",
                 "PUMA", "REGION", "ST")

one_state_schema[subset_cols]$code()

schema(RT = utf8(), SERIALNO = utf8(), DIVISION = int32(), SPORDER =
int32(),
    PUMA = utf8(), REGION = int32(), ST = int32())
```

The last bit of schema manipulation which is useful to know about is how to add or remove items from a schema.

You can add a new item by assigning a data type to a new item in the schema.

```
one_state_schema[["new_var"]] <- float64()

subset_cols <- c("RT", "SERIALNO", "DIVISION", "SPORDER",
                 "PUMA", "REGION", "ST", "new_var")

one_state_schema[subset_cols]

Schema
RT: string
SERIALNO: string
DIVISION: int32
SPORDER: int32
PUMA: string
REGION: int32
ST: int32
new_var: double
```

To remove items from a schema or select a subset, you can create a new schema containing a vector of the names of the desired fields.

```
to_keep <- c("RT", "SERIALNO", "DIVISION", "SPORDER", "PUMA",
             "REGION", "ST", "AGEP", "new_var")
one_state_schema_mini <- one_state_schema[to_keep]
one_state_schema_mini

Schema
RT: string
SERIALNO: string
DIVISION: int32
SPORDER: int32
PUMA: string
REGION: int32
ST: int32
AGEP: int32
new_var: double
```

Alternatively, to just remove items, you can assign the value `NULL` to them, again, just as you could with a list.

```
one_state_schema_mini[["new_var"]] <- NULL
one_state_schema_mini
```

```
Schema
RT: string
SERIALNO: string
DIVISION: int32
SPORDER: int32
PUMA: string
REGION: int32
ST: int32
AGEP: int32
```

### 4.2.3  Writing CSVs

You can write CSV files to disk using `write_csv_arrow()`.

```
# Save `pums_subset` to CSV file
write_csv_arrow(pums_subset, file.path(tmp_dir, "new_pums.csv"))
```

If you're working with large CSV files, you may want to compress them to reduce the amount of space they take up on disk. Arrow automatically detects compression from the file name you give to either the CSV reader or writer, so you can alter the file path to end in `.gz` to save a compressed CSV file.

```
# Write to a gz compressed file
write_csv_arrow(
  pums_subset,
  file.path(tmp_dir, "pums_subset_compressed.csv.gz")
)
```

```
# Read from a gz compressed file
read_csv_arrow(
  file.path(tmp_dir, "pums_subset_compressed.csv.gz")
)
```

Compressed CSVs take up significantly less space on disk, but are slower to read and write. Let's look at an example from the PUMS dataset, using the data for Washington in 2021. We can load in the original data, and then save it to disk, first as an uncompressed CSV and then as a compressed CSV.

```
# Read in the data
washington_2021 <- read_parquet(
  "./data/person/year=2021/location=wa/part-0.parquet"
)
```

```
write_csv_arrow(washington_2021, file.path(tmp_dir, "washington_2021.csv"))
write_csv_arrow(washington_2021, file.path(tmp_dir,
"washington_2021.csv.gz"))
```

The uncompressed CSV is pretty big: 137 MB. However, after the CSV has been compressed, it shrinks down to 19.6 MB.

It's still much larger than a Parquet file with the same data, but not quite as dramatically so.

Although compressing CSVs can lead to much smaller file sizes, they still have issues around data type consistency, and read/write speed. And, on top of that, a compressed CSV loses the one property of CSVs that binary formats don't have: a compressed CSV isn't human readable without doing some extra work to make it so. In the next section, we'll take a look at Parquet format, and discuss how it can bring serious improvements to analytics workflows.

## 4.3 Parquet

As discussed above, Parquet is an open-source standard columnar format supported by arrow and many other big data products. It has many features that make it superior to CSV and other formats.

### 4.3.1 Schema metadata

On of the features of this format is that the schema metadata is saved alongside the data. This means that when you are sharing data between people or programs, there is less chance of errors with data being misinterpreted when it's being read in.

Say we have data like below:

```
numeric_data <- tibble::tibble(
  integers = 1:10,
  doubles = as.numeric(1:10),
  strings = sprintf("%02d", 1:10)
)
numeric_data
```

```
# A tibble: 10 x 3
   integers doubles strings
      <int>   <dbl> <chr>
1         1       1 01
2         2       2 02
3         3       3 03
4         4       4 04
5         5       5 05
6         6       6 06
7         7       7 07
8         8       8 08
9         9       9 09
10       10      10 10
```

In the example below, we create an Arrow Table containing one column of integers, a column of doubles, and a column of strings. We then write them to disk in CSV and Parquet format.

```
numeric_data_schema <- schema(
  integers = int32(),
  doubles = float64(),
  strings = string()
)

numeric_table <- arrow_table(
  numeric_data,
  schema = numeric_data_schema
)

write_csv_arrow(
  numeric_table,
  file.path(tmp_dir, "numeric.csv")
)

write_parquet(
  numeric_table,
  file.path(tmp_dir, "numeric.parquet")
)
```

If we read in the CSV file without providing any information about the schema, arrow will have to guess the schema, and incorrectly infer that the all of the columns are integers.

```
read_csv_arrow(file.path(tmp_dir, "numeric.csv"))
```

```
# A tibble: 10 x 3
   integers doubles strings
      <int>   <int>   <int>
 1        1       1       1
 2        2       2       2
 3        3       3       3
 4        4       4       4
 5        5       5       5
 6        6       6       6
 7        7       7       7
 8        8       8       8
 9        9       9       9
10       10      10      10
```

However, if we read in the Parquet file, the "doubles" column is correctly identified as containing doubles and the "strings" column is correctly identified as containing strings as well as maintains the leading 0.

```
read_parquet(file.path(tmp_dir, "numeric.parquet"))
```

```
# A tibble: 10 x 3
   integers doubles strings
      <int>   <dbl> <chr>
 1        1       1 01
 2        2       2 02
 3        3       3 03
```

```
4          4          4 04
5          5          5 05
6          6          6 06
7          7          7 07
8          8          8 08
9          9          9 09
10         10         10 10
```

The inclusion of the schema metadata in the Parquet files means that these files can easily be shared with less chance of errors from having to guess data types.

### 4.3.2 Preservation of other metadata

Another advantage of Parquet is that it is capable of saving other format-specific metadata. Say you have an SPSS file—in the example below, we'll use one which is included with the haven package.

```
library(haven)

path <- system.file("examples", "iris.sav", package = "haven")
iris_spss <- read_sav(path)
iris_spss
```

```
# A tibble: 150 x 5
   Sepal.Length Sepal.Width Petal.Length Petal.Width Species
          <dbl>       <dbl>        <dbl>       <dbl> <dbl+lbl>
1           5.1         3.5          1.4         0.2 1 [setosa]
2           4.9         3            1.4         0.2 1 [setosa]
3           4.7         3.2          1.3         0.2 1 [setosa]
4           4.6         3.1          1.5         0.2 1 [setosa]
5           5           3.6          1.4         0.2 1 [setosa]
6           5.4         3.9          1.7         0.4 1 [setosa]
7           4.6         3.4          1.4         0.3 1 [setosa]
8           5           3.4          1.5         0.2 1 [setosa]
9           4.4         2.9          1.4         0.2 1 [setosa]
10          4.9         3.1          1.5         0.1 1 [setosa]
# i 140 more rows
```

The `Species` column in this version of the iris dataset is a haven labelled column, a format from SPSS which includes both the value and label. If we were to write this data to a CSV and then read it back into R, we lose the data type and it gets converted to the closest equivalent.

```
library(readr)
tf <- tempfile()
write_csv(iris_spss, tf)
read_csv(tf)
```

```
Rows: 150 Columns: 5
-- Column specification ----------------------------------------
Delimiter: ","
dbl (5): Sepal.Length, Sepal.Width, Petal.Length, Petal.Widt...
```

i Use `spec()` to retrieve the full column specification for this data.
i Specify the column types or set `show_col_types = FALSE` to quiet this
message.

```
# A tibble: 150 x 5
   Sepal.Length Sepal.Width Petal.Length Petal.Width Species
          <dbl>       <dbl>        <dbl>       <dbl>   <dbl>
 1          5.1         3.5          1.4         0.2       1
 2          4.9         3            1.4         0.2       1
 3          4.7         3.2          1.3         0.2       1
 4          4.6         3.1          1.5         0.2       1
 5          5           3.6          1.4         0.2       1
 6          5.4         3.9          1.7         0.4       1
 7          4.6         3.4          1.4         0.3       1
 8          5           3.4          1.5         0.2       1
 9          4.4         2.9          1.4         0.2       1
10          4.9         3.1          1.5         0.1       1
# i 140 more rows
```

However, writing to Parquet and then reading back into R preserves the original data type.

```
tf <- tempfile()
write_parquet(iris_spss, tf)
read_parquet(tf)
```

```
# A tibble: 150 x 5
   Sepal.Length Sepal.Width Petal.Length Petal.Width Species
 *        <dbl>       <dbl>        <dbl>       <dbl> <dbl+lbl>
 1          5.1         3.5          1.4         0.2 1 [setosa]
 2          4.9         3            1.4         0.2 1 [setosa]
 3          4.7         3.2          1.3         0.2 1 [setosa]
 4          4.6         3.1          1.5         0.2 1 [setosa]
 5          5           3.6          1.4         0.2 1 [setosa]
 6          5.4         3.9          1.7         0.4 1 [setosa]
 7          4.6         3.4          1.4         0.3 1 [setosa]
 8          5           3.4          1.5         0.2 1 [setosa]
 9          4.4         2.9          1.4         0.2 1 [setosa]
10          4.9         3.1          1.5         0.1 1 [setosa]
# i 140 more rows
```

This also works for custom classes in R.

Let's take a look at an example of a custom R class for storing fractions. We can define the class and a print method for our fraction class.

```
library(vctrs)
```

```
Attaching package: 'vctrs'
```

```
The following object is masked from 'package:dplyr':

    data_frame
```

The following objects are masked from 'package:arrow':

    field, list_of

```r
# define function to create fraction object
fraction <- function(n = integer(), d = integer()) {

  # ensure inputs are correct types and lengths
  vcc <- vec_cast_common(n, d, .to = integer())
  vrc <- vec_recycle_common(vcc[[1]], vcc[[2]])

  new_rcrd(
    fields = list(numerator = vrc[[1]], denominator = vrc[[2]]),
    class = "fraction"
  )

}


# define a format method for the object
# so we can control how it's printed
format.fraction <- function(x, ...) {
  paste0(field(x, "numerator"), "/", field(x, "denominator"))
}
registerS3method("format", "fraction", format.fraction)

# create and view a fraction object
x <- fraction(1, 5)
x


<fraction[1]>
[1] 1/5
```

This fraction class is a custom class, so it doesn't exist in Arrow or Parquet. However, we can still write this data to Parquet and then back into R, and the type information will be preserved. Let's first set up a tibble containing the values we want to save.

```r
frac_df <- tibble::tibble(
  total = c(2, 2, 7, 9)
)

frac_df$fraction = fraction(
  frac_df$total,
  sum(frac_df$total)
)

frac_df


# A tibble: 4 x 2
  total    fraction
  <dbl> <fraction>
1     2        2/20
2     2        2/20
```

```
3      7       7/20
4      9       9/20
```

If we try to save this data to a CSV, we get an error.

```
tf <- tempfile()
write_csv(frac_df, tf)
```

```
Error in `as.character()`:
! Can't convert `x` <fraction> to <character>.
```

We can, however, save this to Parquet and then read it back into the R session, and the custom class type is retained.

```
tf <- tempfile()
write_parquet(frac_df, tf)
read_parquet(tf)
```

```
# A tibble: 4 x 2
  total      fraction
  <dbl> <fraction>
1     2        2/20
2     2        2/20
3     7        7/20
4     9        9/20
```

This preservation of custom attributes and classes is helpful because it means that we can use custom R packages and save to Parquet files, without having to implement every single specific custom class as a specific Parquet type in the code that reads and writes Parquet. One thing to note is that this preservation of custom attributes works automatically when you write a Parquet file from R and then read it in to R, but it won't work automatically when writing from R and then reading in another language like Python. The custom metadata for each language implementation is stored in a separate location for each language. So while reading data into Python which has a custom class that was created in R, Arrow won't automatically create that same class. However, you still do have access to that metadata under the `metadata` and then `r` attribute if there are details you need to access from Python.

### 4.3.3 File structure and parallelization

Another feature of Parquet is that its files are divided into smaller pieces.

A Parquet file is made up of groups of rows, known as **row groups**. Each of these is divided up into subsections of each column: **column chunks**. These column chunks are then further divided into pages. Earlier, we mentioned that the schema is stored with the data, but there's a lot more metadata in a Parquet file than this. There's also metadata on all of the subcomponents of a Parquet file. The metadata contains information on things like how many rows in that particular subcomponent, and summary statistics about the data contained inside. You can read more about this in the Parquet docs[5].

This micro-level metadata means that software that is designed to work with Parquet, like Arrow, can use this information to work out which data to read in and which data to ignore,

---

[5]https://parquet.apache.org/docs/file-format/metadata/

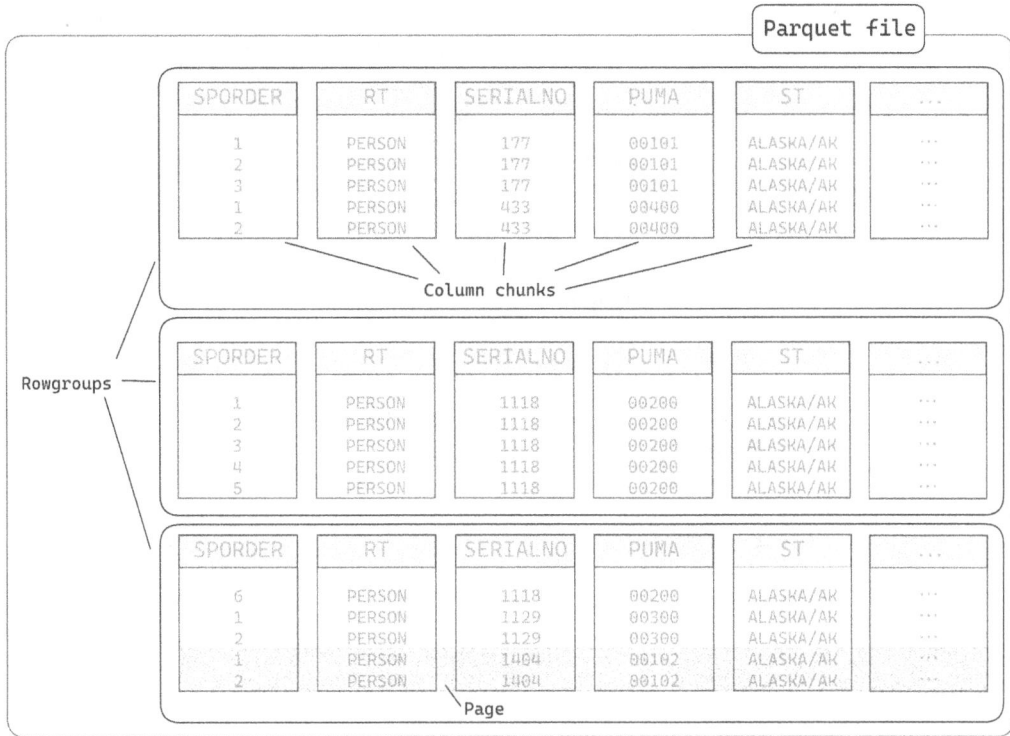

Figure 4.1: Parquet file components

and when combined with the structure here which makes it easier to read things in parallel, can dramatically speed up read time.

### 4.3.4   Columnar format and selective reading

Parquet is a columnar format, which means that data in the same column is stored in adjacent areas of memory. Although row-based format readers typically allow you to specify which columns to read in, this has computational overhead, as the entire row must be read in and the unwanted columns discarded. Parquet's columnar format allows you to read in only the columns you need, and so is much faster when you only require a subset of the data. We'll show some examples that illustrate this efficiency gain in Chapter 6.

### 4.3.5   Dictionary encoding

Parquet's columnar format allows it to take advantage of encoding strategies that can help reduce size on disk. One of these encoding strategies is dictionary encoding; instead of representing every single value in a column, generally Parquet will save the values as key-value pairs, similar to factors. This encoding usually makes the space needed to store string columns much smaller, but there are times when dictionary encoding does not help and in that case we fall back to plain encoding. This fallback happens if the size of the dictionary grows too large, which could happen if there are a large number of distinct values or if the length of each string is large. Note that this is different from Arrow's DictionaryType data type: Parquet's dictionary encoding can be applied to any column type. Parquet's dictionary encoding happens entirely under the hood with arrow so you don't have to decide what is the ideal encoding to store this as—it just happens, unless you actively disable it. We can see its effect by comparing the size of the same Parquet file with and without dictionary encoding. First, let's look at the file size of the Parquet file for Washington in 2021, which was saved with the default setting of using dictionary encoding.

```
wa_21_path <- "./data/person/year=2021/location=wa/part-0.parquet"
fs::file_size(wa_21_path)
```

12.2M

And now let's check out the size of that file if it's saved without dictionary encoding.

```
read_parquet(wa_21_path, as_data_frame = FALSE) |>
  write_parquet(
    file.path(tmp_dir, "pums_subset_no_dict.parquet"),
    use_dictionary = FALSE
  )

fs::file_size(file.path(tmp_dir, "pums_subset_no_dict.parquet"))
```

22.7M

The difference is significant; the file is 1.86 times larger! This isn't the only type of encoding that Parquet uses though; let's take a look next at run-length encoding.

### 4.3.6  Run-length encoding

Writing data to disk with dictionary encoding can help shrink the size of some columns, but there are other aspects of the data that can be taken advantage of. It's not uncommon to find repeated values in the columns of our datasets, and another option for reducing storage space is to use run-length encoding to record the value and how many times it occurs. Let's take a look at the MAR column in the PUMS person dataset subset, representing marital status of respondents.

```
pums_subset_mar <- read_parquet(wa_21_path, col_select = MAR)

count(pums_subset_mar, MAR)
```

```
# A tibble: 5 x 2
  MAR                                    n
  <fct>                              <int>
1 Married                            34829
2 Widowed                             3583
3 Divorced                            7517
4 Separated                            791
5 Never married or under 15 years old 31808
```

There are five different possible values in this column.

In the pseudocode below, we show two different ways we could represent the value "Married" occurring 5 times in a row.

```
["Married ", "Married", "Married", "Married", "Married"]
["Married", 5]
```

In the first version, we store the same value five times, whereas in the second version we just store it once, with the number of times it occurs. The second option takes up fewer characters to represent: this is how run-length encoding works. Run-length encoding is built into Parquet, and we can't turn it off to compare it, but what we can do is reorder our data by the `MAR` column, so that Parquet can take the most advantage of the column ordering, and see what impact it has on the file size.

Let's first take a look at the size of the file containing just the `MAR` column in its original order.

```
unordered_path <- file.path(
  tmp_dir,
  "pums_subset_mar_unordered.parquet"
)

# Write unordered data to a file
write_parquet(pums_subset_mar, unordered_path)

# Get the file of this file
fs::file_size(unordered_path)
```

29.4K

And now, after rearranging the data by the `MAR` column.

```
ordered_path <- file.path(
  tmp_dir,
  "pums_subset_mar_ordered.parquet"
)

# Order data by the `MAR` column
pums_subset_mar_ordered <- pums_subset_mar |>
  arrange(MAR)

# Save this ordered data to a file
write_parquet(pums_subset_mar_ordered, ordered_path)

# Get the file of this file
fs::file_size(ordered_path)
```

589

The file size has now shrunk to be approximately 51.12 times smaller! The effects of run-length encoding are especially noticeable when character columns contain fewer possible values, or data naturally contains repetitions.

### 4.3.7  Compression

Another feature of Parquet is in-built support for compressing data using one of multiple different compression codecs. Generally speaking, all of these codecs reduce the amount of space a Parquet file takes up on disk, and the main differentiation between them relates to how much smaller the resulting file is, and the speed of access when compressing/decompressing the file. Historically, the performance of these codecs has a tradeoff between size and speed: codecs with a higher compression ratio and thus smaller file size tend to result in files which are slower to access than those with a lower compression ratio. More recently, however, benchmarks have shown that the "zstd" codec manages to balance both aspects of performance.

The codecs available depend on your Arrow C++ build. You can use `arrow::arrow_info()` to see a full list of codecs and other capabilities available in your installed version.

Let's take a look at the degree of difference between an uncompressed CSV file, uncompressed Parquet file, compared to "snappy", the default on Linux, and "zstd", one of the current top-performing codecs.

We wrote the files to disk, and then read in just the "AGEP", "COW", and "year" columns. The results can be seen in Table 4.3.

Table 4.3: Comparison of file size, read, and write times for CSV and Parquet

| Format | Size (MB) | Write time (s) | Read time (s) |
|---|---|---|---|
| CSV | 1800 | 24.052 | 10.02 |
| Parquet - uncompressed | 37.1 | 14.89 | 9.215 |
| Parquet - snappy | 35.8 | 15.378 | 10.051 |
| Parquet - zstd | 30.7 | 15.203 | 9.942 |

Ultimately, the different Parquet codecs results in similar performance for read and write times with the data here, though this can vary massively based on the data being written/read. The key points to take away here are:

- you can save a huge amount of space switching from CSV to Parquet
- the default Parquet compression codec is more than adequate in the vast majority of cases
- if you need an extra degree of control it's worth experimenting with the alternatives codecs to see what works best with your data

### 4.3.8　Nested structures

Parquet also has the ability to work with nested structures. The R version of this is list-columns. Using Parquet, we can write list-columns to Parquet files and then read them back into R without having to do any extra additional manual processing.

```
nested_data <- tibble::tibble(
  species = c("cat", "dog", "bird"),
  sounds = list(
    c("meow", "purr", "hiss"),
    c("woof", "bark", "growl"),
    c("tweet", "squawk")
  )
)
```

```
write_parquet(nested_data, "./data/transient_data/nested_data.parquet")
```

```
read_parquet("./data/transient_data/nested_data.parquet")
```

```
# A tibble: 3 x 2
  species          sounds
  <chr>   <list<character>>
1 cat                  [3]
2 dog                  [3]
3 bird                 [2]
```

If we were using CSV format, we would have to flatten the list-columns before saving, and convert them back into a hierarchical structure after loading the file.

---

## 4.4   Example workflow: cleaning the PUMS dataset

Now that we've reviewed the different file formats and options, let's explore a real-world scenario where you would want to use arrow to manipulate individual files.

As is widely stated, the majority of data science work is actually data cleaning. In order to get to the point where we have a nice dataset for analysis, we have to do some work on the raw data. And when data is already spread across multiple files, it is commonplace to have to do transformations to align the files.

The general workflow we'll examine is:

1. `tab <- read_csv_arrow(file, as_data_frame = FALSE)`

2. Do dplyr transformations on the Arrow Table

3. `write_parquet(tab, new_file)`

That is, we'll keep the data in Arrow memory and never pull it into an R data frame. This saves processing time, and it allows us to avoid type conversions between R and Arrow that might lose fidelity.

Let's look at the PUMS dataset. It is a survey, and it has some features commonly found in surveys that need to be cleaned up. For one, the actual row-level data in the survey is encoded based on the type of data it represents.[6] For columns that are numeric, the data is what is in the data file, but characters, factors, and missing values are recorded as integers. These integers must be mapped to values in the codebook, which is distributed with the data and acts as a lookup for what actual value is represented by the integer in the dataset.

For another, the survey questions have changed over time, so data from one year may not line up perfectly with data from other years without some adjustment. Many columns in this dataset require transformation to create a nice consistent dataset to work with.

Let's start with the `COW` variable, which represents class of worker, categorizing people based on their employment status. Using the metadata distributed for PUMS recoding—in the survey world, this is frequently referred to as the *codebook*—we can see that `COW` can take the values 0–9 with the corresponding meaning for the year 2005:

---

[6]Exploring the reasons for this convention is outside of the scope of this book, but it is partly because, historically, folks working with surveys used tools and frameworks that made working with large amounts of data that *wasn't* numeric difficult. However, with modern data tools like arrow, we can effectively and efficiently work with data of all types!

```
codebook |>
  filter(name == "COW")
```

```
    name values_code                       values_label
1   COW            0       Not in universe - missing
2   COW            1               Private for profit
3   COW            2           Private not for profit
4   COW            3                 Local government
5   COW            4                 State government
6   COW            5               Federal government
7   COW            6 Self-employed not incorporated
8   COW            7       Self-employed incorporated
9   COW            8               Without pay--family
10  COW            9                       Unemployed
```

Now let's take a look at the data for the first few rows for the year 2005 and Washington state. First, we read the data in from a single CSV as an Arrow Table, and then we show the first few values for COW.

```
wa_2005 <- read_csv_arrow(
  "data/raw_csvs/person/2005/wa/ss05pwa.csv",
  as_data_frame = FALSE
)
```

```
wa_2005 |>
  select(COW) |>
  head() |>
  collect()
```

```
# A tibble: 6 x 1
    COW
  <int>
1    NA
2     1
3     6
4     1
5     3
6     1
```

We see values like 1, 6, 1, 3, etc. We ultimately want these to match up to the labels "Private for profit", "Self-employed not incorporated", "Private for profit", "Local government", etc. One way that we can do this is by using a join, matching on the value codes in the codebook to pull in the value labels:

```
wa_2005 |>
  left_join(
    filter(codebook, name == "COW"),
    by = c("COW" = "values_code")
  ) |>
  mutate(COW_label = values_label, .keep = "unused") |>
  select(sporder, SERIALNO, PUMA, ST, PWGTP, COW, COW_label) |>
  head() |>
```

```
  collect()
```

```
# A tibble: 6 x 7
  sporder SERIALNO  PUMA    ST PWGTP   COW COW_label
    <int>    <int> <int> <int> <int> <int> <chr>
1       1       86   700    53    57     1 Private for profit
2       2       86   700    53    45     6 Self-employed not in~
3       1      101  2009    53   201     1 Private for profit
4       2      101  2009    53   191     3 Local government
5       1      132  2006    53    91     1 Private for profit
6       1      183  1404    53    49     1 Private for profit
```

Above, we kept both `COW` and `COW_label` to illustrate the mapping, but we could replace it like so:

```
wa_2005 |>
  left_join(
    filter(codebook, name == "COW"),
    by = c("COW" = "values_code")
  ) |>
  mutate(COW = values_label, .keep = "unused") |>
  select(sporder, SERIALNO, PUMA, ST, PWGTP, COW, AGEP) |>
  head() |>
  collect()
```

```
# A tibble: 6 x 7
  sporder SERIALNO  PUMA    ST PWGTP COW                     AGEP
    <int>    <int> <int> <int> <int> <chr>                  <int>
1       1    27046  1803    53   103 Local government          46
2       1    27172   200    53   105 Private for profit        29
3       2    27172   200    53   106 Self-employed not in~     27
4       1    27284  1600    53    88 Local government          39
5       1    27332   800    53   179 Private for profit        33
6       2    27332   800    53   120 Private for profit        36
```

We can do this with multiple variables at once, and when we're happy with the result, we can skip the `collect()` step and just pipe the transformed data to `write_parquet()`:

```
wa_2005 |>
  left_join(
    filter(codebook, name == "COW"),
    by = c("COW" = "values_code")
  ) |>
  mutate(COW = values_label, .keep = "unused") |>
  left_join(
    filter(codebook, name == "JWTR"),
    by = c("JWTR" = "values_code")
  ) |>
  mutate(JWTR = values_label, .keep = "unused") |>
  write_parquet("wa_2005.parquet")
```

This will take the Table, which was read from the CSVs, and write out a Parquet file without ever holding the data in an R data frame.

From here, we could recode each of the columns using the codebook and write out cleaned Parquet files. We go from reading the data into Arrow tables and then using Arrow's data processing abilities to transform the data from the raw, survey-specific format into one that is more natural to work with.

For this book, we've gone ahead and processed all of the data for PUMS from 2005 to 2022, both the person-level and the household-level data. This is, of course, slightly more involved than we show here since we have hundreds of variables to join and there are subtle changes to the schema of the raw data from one year to the next. But the concept and approach we show here is the same. If you're curious to learn more, see Section A.2.1.

## 4.5   Summary

In this chapter, we examined the different file formats which are supported by Arrow and compared their advantages and disadvantages, as well as discussing how they work. If you're looking for a TL;DR about what format to store your data in, as of the writing of this book we recommend Parquet. There are very specific other circumstances where Arrow IPC or CSV might be required, but the benefits of Parquet make it the right choice in the vast majority of circumstances.

We took a look at functions for reading and writing individual files into memory as Arrow Tables. In the next chapter, we'll take a look at Arrow Datasets: a powerful concept for working with datasets split across multiple files.

# 5

## Datasets

The examples in Chapter 4 discussed working with data stored in single files, which can be manipulated in R as data frames or Arrow Tables. These are helpful when you have data which is small enough to fit in your R session, but what about when it isn't? This is when Arrow Datasets are needed.

You've examples of working with Arrow Datasets in Chapters 2, and now we're going to dive deeper into the details. In this chapter, we're going to take a look at exactly what Datasets *are*, how they work, working with non-default options, and how to really optimize for performance.

One note before we get started: we'll use "Datasets" to refer to the concept of an Arrow Dataset object itself, and the word "dataset" if we're just talking about a collection of data in a more general way.

Datasets don't represent data loaded into memory, but instead contains information about:

* where the files in the Dataset are located
* what format the files are in
* what the schema of those files is—the column names and types

If we take a look at the PUMS person dataset, we can see that it contains a total of 832 files, which are in Parquet format.

```
library(arrow)
library(dplyr)
pums_person <- open_dataset("./data/person")
pums_person
```

```
FileSystemDataset with 884 Parquet files
311 columns
SPORDER: int32
RT: dictionary<values=string, indices=int32>
SERIALNO: string
PUMA: string
ST: string
ADJUST: int32
PWGTP: int32
AGEP: int32
CIT: dictionary<values=string, indices=int32>
COW: dictionary<values=string, indices=int32>
DDRS: bool
DEYE: bool
DOUT: bool
DPHY: bool
```

DOI: 10.1201/9781032663197-5

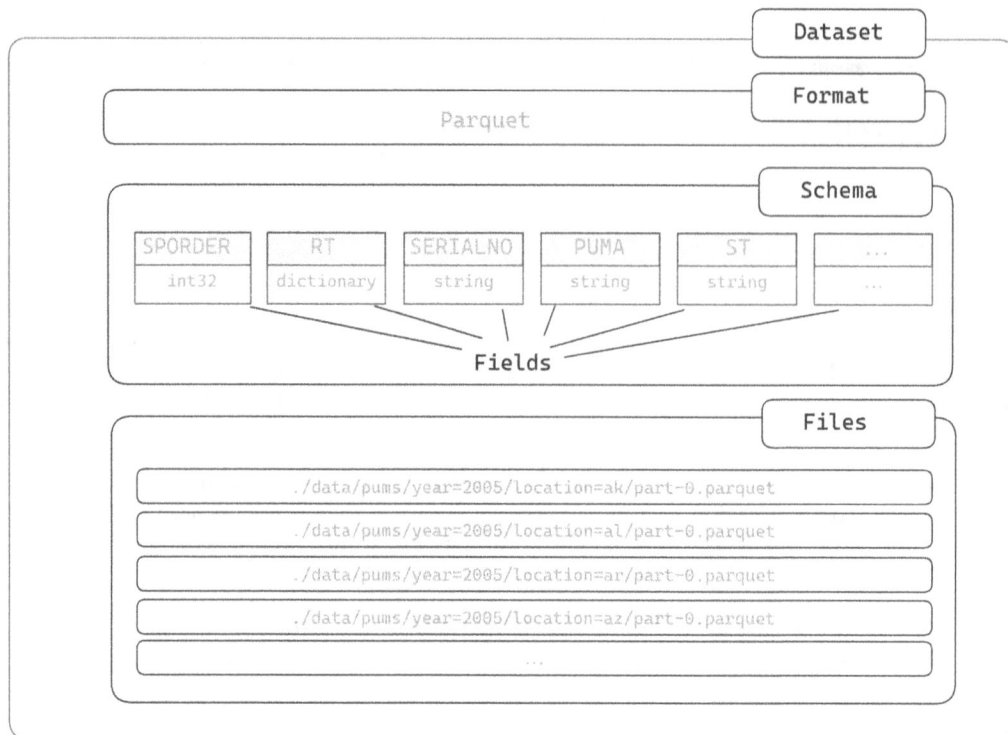

Figure 5.1: Dataset components

```
DREM: bool
DWRK: bool
ENG: dictionary<values=string, indices=int32>
FER: bool
GCL: bool
GCM: dictionary<values=string, indices=int32>
...
291 more columns
Use `schema()` to see entire schema
```

We can use the `files` attribute to look at the locations of the first 10 files in the dataset.

```
pums_person$files[1:10]
```

```
 [1] "./data/person/year=2005/location=ak/part-0.parquet"
 [2] "./data/person/year=2005/location=al/part-0.parquet"
 [3] "./data/person/year=2005/location=ar/part-0.parquet"
 [4] "./data/person/year=2005/location=az/part-0.parquet"
 [5] "./data/person/year=2005/location=ca/part-0.parquet"
 [6] "./data/person/year=2005/location=co/part-0.parquet"
 [7] "./data/person/year=2005/location=ct/part-0.parquet"
 [8] "./data/person/year=2005/location=dc/part-0.parquet"
 [9] "./data/person/year=2005/location=de/part-0.parquet"
[10] "./data/person/year=2005/location=fl/part-0.parquet"
```

You may notice that the directories in which the files are stored related to variables in the dataset: `year` and `location`. This way of structuring data is known as partitioning, and we'll be looking at this in more detail in a later section.

There are a few important ways in which an Arrow Dataset is different to an Arrow Table:

- Tables contain data in memory, whereas Datasets are a representation of the data on disk without being loaded into memory
- Datasets do not have an inherent concept of ordering as there is no guarantee as to the order in which files in a Dataset will be read in

More importantly, there are several ways that an Arrow Dataset is similar to an Arrow Table:

- You can use familiar dplyr syntax to construct and execute queries using both
- They both use the standard, modern, and rich Arrow type system
- They both can be passed to other systems that know about the Arrow format without serialization, either using more processing in the arrow R package, or using other projects such as DuckDB or pyarrow

There are two typical workflows that we see people using when working with larger-than-memory datasets, depending on whether their focus is data engineering or data analysis.

## 5.1  ETL

**ETL** stands for *Extract, Transform, and Load*, and it describes a data-engineering process in which data is ingested from one or more sources, some transformations are applied to it, and then it's loaded into some sort of data repository or warehouse ready for analysis. It is particularly useful when the process by which data is generated involves appending new rows of data, such as web traffic logs. As we have discussed before, row-oriented data stores are not optimized for analytic queries, so ETL is useful to process the raw data into a form that is better suited to analysis.

In the context of arrow, you'd typically start with raw data which is larger than memory, potentially modify it, and write it out in a more helpful format with partitions that are useful for analyzing. One important thing to know here is that because arrow writes datasets one piece at a time, you don't have to worry about your dataset being larger than memory. You can use the same code that works on data in memory—which has quick feedback and you can see if things are going well—as you do for the full dataset that might take many minutes or even hours to process and is impossible to load into memory all at once.

Partitioning here is not technically critical, but this is the stage where it is easiest to introduce or change a dataset's partitioning strategy. We'll talk more on how to pick a strategy later in the chapter.

```
my_dataset <- open_csv_dataset(path = "./data/my-oversized-csv.csv")

my_dataset |>
  mutate(year = year(datetime), month = month(datetime)) |>
  write_dataset(
    path = "./data/my-much-nicer-parquet-dataset",
    partitioning = c("year", "month")
  )
```

## 5.2   Analysis oriented workflow

The other workflow where we work with larger-than-memory datasets is when scanning the dataset and aggregating values—the stage that may happen after having done ETL. Effective use of partitioning is important here. In an analysis-focused workflow, you may want to do things like calculating grouped summaries. For example, we can compute the average commute time in Washington by year from the census data:

```
open_dataset("./data/person") |>
  filter(location == "wa") |>
  group_by(year) |>
  summarize(
    avg_commute = sum(JWMNP * PWGTP, na.rm = TRUE) / sum(PWGTP)
  ) |>
  arrange(desc(year)) |>
  collect()
```

```
# A tibble: 17 x 2
    year avg_commute
   <int>       <dbl>
 1  2022        10.3
 2  2021         9.36
 3  2019        13.2
 4  2018        12.9
 5  2017        12.7
 6  2016        12.5
 7  2015        12.1
 8  2014        11.9
 9  2013        11.4
10  2012        11.4
11  2011        10.9
12  2010        10.7
13  2009        11.1
14  2008        11.8
15  2007        11.8
16  2006        11.4
17  2005        11.2
```

In this chapter, we'll be looking at topics relevant to both of these workflows, and discussing the different ways you can work with datasets with arrow.

## 5.3   Functions for reading and writing datasets

We've already looked at some examples using the `open_dataset()` function. The previous examples used Arrow and Parquet datasets, but Arrow supports the same formats for datasets that it does for working with individual files: CSV and similar text-delimited formats, Parquet, Arrow IPC format, and line-delimited JSON.

The different functions for reading and writing datasets are shown in Table 5.1 below.

Table 5.1: Functions for reading and writing datasets

| Format | Reading | Writing |
|---|---|---|
| Parquet | open_dataset() | write_dataset() |
| CSV (or other delimited file) | open_dataset(..., format = "csv"), open_csv_dataset(), open_delim_dataset() | write_dataset(..., format = "csv") |
| Line-delimited JSON | open_dataset(..., format = "json") | (Not supported) |

The convenience functions `open_csv_dataset()` and `open_delim_dataset()` are wrappers around `open_dataset(..., format = "csv")` but using arguments which match `read_csv_arrow()` and `read_delim_arrow()` to make it easier to switch between working with individual files and multifile datasets by just changing the function call.

In this chapter we'll focus on the practicalities of working with different formats in the context of Arrow Datasets, but if you want a reminder of the general advantages and disadvantages of working with the different file formats, see Chapter 4. As a reminder, we recommend working with Parquet format if you can. Parquet files are already smaller and faster to work with than text-based, delimited files, but there are further advantages of using Parquet when working with multifile datasets. Because Parquet files contain metadata, Arrow can make use of this information when working with datasets. This metadata contains information about rows and columns, which means that when using data pipelines using `dplyr::filter()` or `dplyr::select()`, Arrow can use the metadata to work out which data to scan instead of having to check the values in every single file or smaller component. This can significantly speed up analyses of larger datasets.

## 5.4 Partitioning

We have already been working with partitioned data: the data in the PUMS person dataset has been partitioned based on the "year" and "location" columns.

Partitioning is where groups of rows of data have been saved to separate files. These separate files are saved in directories, where each directory represents the rows of the data where a particular column has a particular value.

You're not limited to a single level of directories; you can have multiple nested levels. The PUMS person dataset has "year" at the top level and "location" in the next level down. What this means is that there are 17 directories at the top level: one for each of the years in the dataset, which range from 2005 to 2022. Within each of these year directories, there are 52 subdirectories; one for each of the different locations. In total, we end up with 884

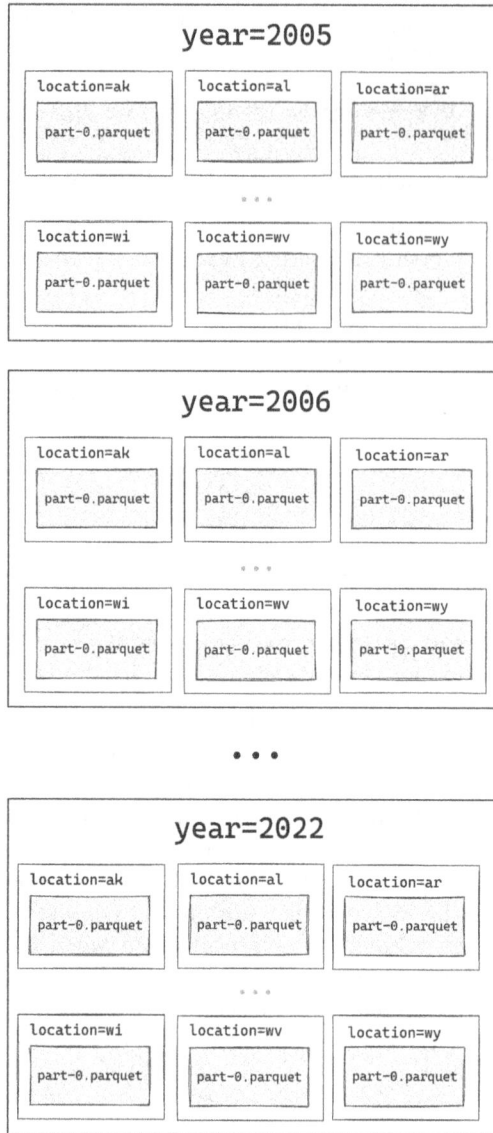

Figure 5.2: Folder and file structure of a partitioned dataset

bottom-level directories, and inside each of them there is a single Parquet file for each year/location combination.[1]

One thing to note is that the data in the column that we partition by is *not included* in the columns within the Parquet files themselves. This is partially to conserve data: rather than include the same value over and over again inside the Parquet files, it is put once

---

[1]Though it is typical to have a single Parquet file in each directory, that is not a requirement. Arrow will read any files that are in that folder and join them together as if they were in one file. Depending on the structure of your data this might be because of how it was batched when it was written, but generally we can ignore that it happens.

in the directory name. More importantly[2] though, this prevents the possibility of having two columns which disagree with each other. What should happen if the directory says `year=2008`, but the column `year` in the file is all 2020?

There are many reasons to work with partitioned data—you may have received the data in this format, or you may have chosen to partition your data to take advantage of improved performance on data analysis and smaller file sizes.

In the next section we'll talk about how to work with partitioned data.

### 5.4.1  Hive and non-Hive partitioned data

Writing the data to directories which are given names based on the column name and value as key-value pairs is called **Hive-style partitioning**, named after Apache Hive, where this first was introduced as a convention.

Arrow will automatically look for Hive-style partitions when passed in the name of a directory. One of the benefits of using Hive-style partitioning is that the column names are encoded into the directory names themselves. This means that when we open our Parquet format PUMS dataset, we don't need to do anything extra for the `year` and `location` values in the directory names to be recognized as part of the dataset schema.

```
open_dataset("./data/person")
```

What if the data we are working with isn't stored with Hive-style partitions? We might need to work with data which is partitioned, but the directory names are just the values of the partitioning column without the name, for example, a directory simply called 2022 instead of `year=2022`, and so on for the other years. This is sometimes referred to as non-Hive-partitioned data.

Let's take a look at an example of this, and write the dataset to a new directory, but this time, using just the value of year in the directory name. We can do this by passing in the parameter `hive_style = FALSE` into our call to `write_dataset()`.

```
tmp_dir <- "./data/transient_data/"
open_dataset("./data/person") |>
  write_dataset(
    file.path(tmp_dir, "person_non_hive"),
    partitioning = "year",
    hive_style = FALSE
  )
```

If we inspect the content of the new directory, we can see that the filenames indeed are just the year numbers but without the `year` identifier.

```
fs::dir_ls(file.path(tmp_dir, "person_non_hive"))
```

```
./data/transient_data/person_non_hive/2005
./data/transient_data/person_non_hive/2006
./data/transient_data/person_non_hive/2007
./data/transient_data/person_non_hive/2008
```

---

[2]In fact, with modern compression algorithms and modern data formats like Parquet, a column that has a single value would end up taking very little space. This was much more of an issue when working with CSVs and other formats that couldn't take advantage of per-column compression.

```
./data/transient_data/person_non_hive/2009
./data/transient_data/person_non_hive/2010
./data/transient_data/person_non_hive/2011
./data/transient_data/person_non_hive/2012
./data/transient_data/person_non_hive/2013
./data/transient_data/person_non_hive/2014
./data/transient_data/person_non_hive/2015
./data/transient_data/person_non_hive/2016
./data/transient_data/person_non_hive/2017
./data/transient_data/person_non_hive/2018
./data/transient_data/person_non_hive/2019
./data/transient_data/person_non_hive/2021
./data/transient_data/person_non_hive/2022
```

Now if we open this dataset like before, `year` is no longer automatically recognized as a column in the dataset.

```
ds <- open_dataset(file.path(tmp_dir, "person_non_hive"))
```

To get Arrow to recognize that we want to include the directory name as a column in our dataset, we need to tell it do this by manually specifying the `partitioning` argument in our call to `open_dataset()`.

```
ds <- open_dataset(
  file.path(tmp_dir, "person_non_hive"),
  partitioning = "year"
)
```

Because this filesystem path is text-based, Arrow must do type inference on this path to guess what type the partition variable should be. Arrow tries its best to get this right, but sometimes you might want to add the data type for the partitioned columns. This can be useful if you have a type that looks like a number, but should actually be a character (like we discussed in the previous chapter on files and formats). Additionally, it can be helpful for specifying different data size of integers like we do here. For example, the maximum 16-bit integer is 32767, and that can safely accommodate `year` for the foreseeable future, so there's no reason to store it as a 32- or 64-bit integer. This is very similar to how we would specify data types when creating a schema. We do this by using the `hive_partition()` function, and we specify the column name and type:

```
ds <- open_dataset(
  file.path(tmp_dir, "person_non_hive"),
  partitioning = hive_partition(year = int16())
)
```

The use of Hive-style partitioning when saving datasets is a helpful way of ensuring that we automatically read in the partitions as variables, without additional manual intervention. Hive-style partitioning is also a common enough standard in data systems these days that it has become something of a standard itself.

### 5.4.2   Partitioning data using `dplyr::group_by()`

In the examples above, we showed examples of writing partitioned data by using the `partitioning` argument to `write_dataset()`. Alternatively, if you have data which has been grouped using `dplyr::group_by()`, arrow will automatically write the data to partitions based on this grouping. For example, if we wanted to partition the PUMS dataset solely on year (but not location), we could open the dataset, use `group_by()` to change the partitioning, and then write a new copy to a new directory.

```
open_dataset("./data/person") |>
  group_by(year) |>
  write_dataset(file.path(tmp_dir, "person_year"))
```

### 5.4.3 Partitioning data with a new column

Another common use case is to create a completely new variable to use to partition our data. For example, what if we want to partition the dataset based on different age groups? We can create a new column in our data using `group_by()` and `case_when()` to create this new variable based on the values in the `AGEP` column. We can then write the new dataset to disk using `write_dataset()`, specifying the path where we want to save the data, and which variables to partition on.

```
open_dataset("./data/person") |>
  group_by(
    year,
    location,
    age_group = case_when(
      AGEP < 25 ~ "Under 25",
      AGEP < 35 ~ "25-34",
      AGEP < 45 ~ "35-44",
      AGEP < 55 ~ "45-54",
      AGEP < 65 ~ "55-64",
      TRUE ~ "65+"
    )
  ) |>
  write_dataset(path = file.path(tmp_dir, "person-age-partitions"))
```

### 5.4.4 Custom filenames

By default, Arrow will write Parquet files in the form: `part-{#}.parquet`. You can also control the file name using the `basename_template` parameter.

```
open_dataset("./data/person") |>
  filter(year >= 2020) |>
  write_dataset(
    file.path(tmp_dir, "person_starting_2020_fn"),
    basename_template = "data_{i}.parquet"
  )
```

This has now updated the name of the saved files.

```
fs::dir_ls(
  file.path(tmp_dir, "person_starting_2020_fn"),
  recurse = TRUE
)
```

```
./data/transient_data/person_starting_2020_fn/data_0.parquet
```

### 5.4.5   Writing to existing partitions

In all of the examples so far, we've been writing data to different directories each time. If we were to use existing directories, there are different values which can be specified to the `existing_data_behavior` option which change how Arrow behaves when it encounters data already present in those directories:

- `"overwrite"`: the default value; replaces any files with the same name as files to be written but leave any extra files there
- `"delete_matching"`: entirely deletes any data in any partitions which are going to be written to
- `"error"`: raise an error message if existing data is found

Depending on your data and what you're trying to do, it's important to consider which of these options is the best fit for you if writing to directories which already contain data. If you are expecting to be replacing all of the data in a directory which currently has 3 Parquet files in it, but you only write the first one this time, you will have extra rows in your dataset from the second and third Parquet files added back to your dataset when you read it.

In this case, if you'd rather completely delete any existing data in the directory you want to write to, you should set `existing_data_behavior` to `delete_matching` and any existing data in that directory will be removed.

```
open_dataset("./data/person") |>
  filter(year >= 2020) |>
  write_dataset(
    file.path(tmp_dir, "person_starting_2020"),
    existing_data_behavior = "delete_matching"
  )
```

Also, consider starting fresh with a new directory when you want to be sure there are no clashes or surprises using the `"error"` key that will let you know if something is there already.

```
open_dataset("./data/person") |>
  filter(year >= 2020) |>
  write_dataset(
    file.path(tmp_dir, "person_starting_2020"),
    existing_data_behavior = "error"
  )
```

### 5.4.6   Filename-based partitioning

While data partitioned by directory is simpler to deal with, Arrow also supports working with data partitioned by filename. For example, perhaps you have a dataset where each file contains data for a single day, and the filename is the date in YYYY-MM-DD format.

```
fs::dir_ls(file.path(tmp_dir, "logs"))
```

```
./data/transient_data/logs/logs_2023-12-01.parquet
./data/transient_data/logs/logs_2024-01-01.parquet
./data/transient_data/logs/logs_2024-02-01.parquet
```

You can use the `add_filename()` function to add a column to your dataset which contains the filename of the file that each row of data came from. You can then further manipulate this column to extract just the date component of the filename.

We'll do this one step at a time. First we call `add_filename()` to create the new column containing the filename. Then, we use `stringr::str_remove()` to get rid of the path to the file and the `logs_` prefix. Next we use `stringr::str_remove()` again, to remove the `.parquet` suffix. We then use `ymd()` to convert the filename to a date type, and finally use `year()` to extract the year component of the date. Now we can use this new year column to partition our dataset.

```
open_dataset(file.path(tmp_dir, "logs")) |>
  mutate(file = add_filename()) |>
  mutate(file = str_remove(file, "^.*/logs_")) |>
  mutate(file = str_remove(file, ".parquet$")) |>
  mutate(year_month = str_remove(file, "-..$")) |>
  write_dataset(
    file.path(tmp_dir, "logs_repartitioned"),
    partitioning = "year_month"
  )
```

```
./data/transient_data/logs_repartitioned/year_month=2023-12
./data/transient_data/logs_repartitioned/year_month=2024-01
./data/transient_data/logs_repartitioned/year_month=2024-02
```

### 5.4.7 Partitions containing NA values

Now you've seen that partitioning creates different directories based on the values in the column that you partition your data on, but what about if that column contains NA values? Let's take a look at what happens. We'll create a simple toy example to demonstrate.

```
data <- tibble::tibble(
  x = 1:6,
  y = c(rep("group1", 5), NA)
)
```

```
partition_with_na_path <- file.path(
  tmp_dir,
  "na-partition-default"
)
```

```
write_dataset(data, partition_with_na_path, partitioning = "y")
fs::dir_ls(partition_with_na_path)
```

```
./data/transient_data/na-partition-default/y=__HIVE_DEFAULT_PARTITION__
./data/transient_data/na-partition-default/y=group1
```

The data is being saved, as expected, in Hive-style directories, using the key=value pairing. However, when there is an NA value in the grouping column, the value part of the directory name is saved as `"__HIVE_DEFAULT_PARTITION__"`. If you would rather specify your own replacement value, you can use the `hive_partition()` function to have more control of your data. You'll need to supply the data types of the partition variable too, and then pass in your chosen default value as the `null_fallback` parameter.

```
partition_with_custom_na_path <- file.path(
  tmp_dir,
  "na-partition-custom"
)

write_dataset(
  data,
  partition_with_custom_na_path,
  partitioning = hive_partition(
    y = string(), null_fallback = "no_group"
  )
)

fs::dir_ls(partition_with_custom_na_path)
```

```
./data/transient_data/na-partition-custom/y=group1
./data/transient_data/na-partition-custom/y=no_group
```

## 5.5   How partitioning affects performance

Now we've looked at different ways of creating partitioning, it's time to take a look at the impact it has on performance.

We're going to create four example datasets to use to demonstrate this:

1. One big file: all of the PUMS person-level data stored in a single 7.6 GB Parquet file
2. Year-partitioned data: partitioning the PUMS person-level data by year
3. Year and location-partitioned data: partitioning the PUMS person-level data by both year and location—this is the dataset we've already been working with in most of our examples so far
4. Year, location, and age-group partitioned data: partitioning the PUMS person-level data by year, location, and a new variable we're going to create called age_group.

Here's the code to create these datasets.

```
# 1. Everything on one big file
open_dataset("./data/person") |>
  write_dataset(file.path(tmp_dir, "person_onefile"))

pums_one_big_file <- open_dataset(
  file.path(tmp_dir, "person_onefile")
)

# 2. Partitioned by year
open_dataset("./data/person") |>
  write_dataset(
```

```
    file.path(tmp_dir, "person_year"),
    partitioning = "year"
)

pums_by_year <- open_dataset(
  file.path(tmp_dir, "person_year")
)

# 3. Partitioned by year and location
# We don't need to create a new dataset here as
# this already is the structure of the data
pums_by_year_location <- open_dataset("./data/person")

# 4. Partitioned by year, location, and new column age_group

open_dataset("./data/person") |>
  mutate(
    age_group = case_when(
      AGEP < 25 ~ "Under 25",
      AGEP < 35 ~ "25-34",
      AGEP < 45 ~ "35-44",
      AGEP < 55 ~ "45-54",
      AGEP < 65 ~ "55-64",
      TRUE ~ "65+"
    )
  ) |>
  write_dataset(
    path = file.path(tmp_dir, "person_year_location_age"),
    partitioning = c("year", "location", "age_group")
  )

pums_by_year_location_age <- open_dataset(
  file.path(tmp_dir, "person_year_location_age")
)
```

Table 5.2 shows how many files in each dataset, as well as the minimum, maximum, and median file size.

Table 5.2: Summary statistics around file sizes of partitioned datasets

| Dataset | # of Files | Min size (MB) | Median size (MB) | Max size (MB) |
|---|---|---|---|---|
| pums_one_big_file | 1 | 7786.3 | 7786.3 | 7786.3 |
| pums_by_year | 34 | 0.1 | 211.8 | 493 |
| pums_by_year_location | 1785 | 0.1 | 0.1 | 56.1 |
| pums_by_year_location_age | 14124 | 0.1 | 0.4 | 17.6 |

### 5.5.1   Querying across all data

First, let's try running query which just requires filtering the data by one of the partition variables, year, to only include the data from 2018 onwards, and then calculate a summary based on the variable JWMNP, which contains data about commute times, and isn't a partition variable.

```
open_dataset("<path/to/data>") |>
  filter(year >= 2018) |>
  summarise(
    mean_commute = sum(JWMNP * PWGTP, na.rm = TRUE) / sum(PWGTP)
  ) |>
  collect()
```

Table 5.3 shows the results of running that query on Nic's laptop, with the datasets we created earlier.

Table 5.3: Time taken to run a query unrelated to dataset partitions, with different partitioning structures

| Dataset | Query completion time (s) |
| --- | --- |
| pums_one_big_file | 2.2 |
| pums_by_year | 1.0 |
| pums_by_year_location | 1.8 |
| pums_by_year_location_age | 6.5 |

In this case, the fastest query time was on the dataset which was partitioned solely by year, the only partition column used in the query. In the case of storing the data in one big file, Arrow has to open the file and use the metadata to work out which of the contents to use in the analysis. Partitioning by year means that Arrow can entirely disregard the partitions containing years that aren't relevant here. When we say "entirely disregard", we mean that it doesn't even read any part of the Parquet file at all during the query—not even the header.

We can also see from this that having additional unnecessary partitions will slow things down: the dataset partitioned by all of year, location, and age, was by far the slowest.

### 5.5.2   Querying with results grouped by partition variables

Above we saw that a query that uses the only partitioning columns shows the best performance compared to other partitioning strategies. So next let's take a look at how the query times compare when all three of the partition variables are relevant to the query. We can set up another query in which we group our results by our three partition variables.

```
open_dataset("<path/to/data>") |>
  filter(year >= 2012) |>
  mutate(
    age_group = case_when(
      AGEP < 25 ~ "Under 25",
      AGEP < 35 ~ "25-34",
      AGEP < 45 ~ "35-44",
```

```
      AGEP < 55 ~ "45-54",
      AGEP < 65 ~ "55-64",
      TRUE ~ "65+"
    )
  ) |>
  group_by(year, age_group, location) |>
  summarise(
    mean_commute = sum(JWMNP * PWGTP, na.rm = TRUE) / sum(PWGTP)
  ) |>
  collect()
```

We ran it again on Nic's laptop, and the results are shown in Table 5.4.

Table 5.4: Time taken to run a query relating to dataset partitions, with different partition-ing structures

| Dataset | Query completion time (s) |
|---|---|
| pums_one_big_file | 4.6 |
| pums_by_year | 3.2 |
| pums_by_year_location | 3.3 |
| pums_by_year_location_age | 11.5 |

The final query was tested without the call to `mutate()` as the column already existed as a partition, but this made little difference to the overall time—too many partitions create an overhead because Arrow has to open too many different files. There's a relatively fixed cost to opening and reading any Parquet file, no matter how big that file is. When we have many small files, we have to spend more time reading in the relatively fixed size of the Parquet header data and metadata, on top of the time spent reading the actual data. When thinking about how we organize our partitions, there is a balance to be struck between how many files there are to read in, and avoiding reading in more of the data than we need to.

The specific contents of the query we want to run on the data is also important here. One key difference between this query and the previous one is that the partition variables were all used in calls to `group_by()` and not `filter()`.

### 5.5.3 Querying with partition variables used to filter the data

Let's try one more time to see what happens when we need to filter on all three variables.

```
open_dataset("<path/to/data>") |>
  mutate(
    age_group = case_when(
      AGEP < 25 ~ "Under 25",
      AGEP < 35 ~ "25-34",
      AGEP < 45 ~ "35-44",
      AGEP < 55 ~ "45-54",
      AGEP < 65 ~ "55-64",
      TRUE ~ "65+"
    )
  ) |>
```

```
filter(
  year >= 2012,
  location %in% c("ny", "ca"),
  age_group == "Under 25"
) |>
group_by(year, location, age_group) |>
summarise(
  mean_commute = sum(JWMNP * PWGTP, na.rm = TRUE) / sum(PWGTP)
) |>
collect()
```

Once again, we removed the call to `mutate()` for the dataset which already had the `age_group` partition variable.

Table 5.5: Time taken to run a query which filters on dataset partitions, with different partitioning structures

| Dataset | Query completion time (s) |
|---|---|
| pums_one_big_file | 3.6 |
| pums_by_year | 2.5 |
| pums_by_year_location | 2.2 |
| pums_by_year_location_age | 0.8 |

This time the differences were a lot more marked! As you can see in Table 5.5, it's the variables most commonly used for filtering which partitions have the most impact on.

We don't recommend repartitioning your data every time you want to run a query on your dataset, as the overhead of time spent rewriting the data to disk means it probably won't be worth it. What we'd recommend instead is thinking about which variables you use most frequently in calls to `filter()` in your analyses, and store your data in partitions based on these variables.

As we saw above, reading only the data from disk that is important for a query is the fastest way to process that data. What this means is that if we know that specific Parquet files only include rows that we don't care about—because they don't match the conditions in the filter—then skipping over them entirely is best. Partitioning based on common filters means that arrow can skip over files entirely when they are in partitioned like this.

That said, it's important not to create too many files, because for each Parquet file read in from disk, there is a relatively fixed amount of metadata that must be read alongside the data. This metadata includes things like the schema of the data and other statistics about the data in the file. The more Parquet files you have, the more of this fixed, extra information has to be read in. Having files smaller than 20 MB will typically mean considerably more reading of that metadata compared to reading actual data itself. Equally, having files larger than 2 GB means that you're no longer able to take advantage of Arrow's ability to read multiple files in parallel.

The number of levels of partitioning is also important. While writing this book, we tried to test out an example which used an extra level of partitioning as well as `year`, `location`, and `age_group`, as well as partitioning on the `PUMA` (Public use microdata area code) column, which has thousands of unique values. However, it took over 3 hours to write to disk, produced around 800,000 files, and took up 81 GB on disk. The sheer quantity of files which needed writing, and the overhead in terms of storage size (and also query time if analyzed later) caused by the associated file headers and metadata, meant that it just wasn't feasible to include this, even as an example!

Getting partitioning correct is a balancing act and there is no single configuration that will work for all data and all queries. The unique characteristics of your data and your typical queries will determine the best partitioning for your data.

### 5.5.4 Tuning writing parameters

There are more options to further control partition-writing behavior. The default values for these options are good for most workflows. However, in some circumstances, you might want to change them to get optimum performance. If you are seeing poor performance, or your data happens to be peculiar (you have a huge number of columns, you have a huge number of partition values, etc.) you might find tuning these values can improve performance.

The sections below contain options you can tune and are ordered from most likely to need tuning to least likely. For some of these settings, if you find yourself needing to tune it, that's actually an indication that your data setup is not optimal for your situation. This most commonly happens when you have too many and too small partitions. You will think you need to adjust these values to get good write performance, but as we saw above, having too many and too small partitions hurts the performance of reading and analysis as well. In those situations, rather than tune these settings, it's better to adjust your partitioning strategy.

#### 5.5.4.1 `max_rows_per_file`

The maximum number of rows in each file.

If you have particularly large partitions, it can sometimes be helpful to limit the number of rows in each Parquet file. This is helpful if you're finding you are having memory issues while writing datasets because it will write to disk a chunk of data even if it's not the full partition.

#### 5.5.4.2 `max_rows_per_group`

The maximum rows allowed in a single group and when this number of rows is exceeded, it is split and the next set of rows is written to the next group.

Arrow tries to write as large row groups as possible—the default maximum number of rows is just over one million. Row groups of this size are usually a good thing because they provide a balance between containing enough data to make compression effective and still having the benefit of being able to skip row groups when reading data based on the group-level statistics.

If your data has a very large number of columns, or contains data that is particularly large (e.g. a large number of long character strings in each column), you might want to reduce this number to make your row groups smaller.

#### 5.5.4.3 `min_rows_per_group`

Write the row groups to the disk only when this number of rows or more have accumulated.

By default, any number of rows can be written to a row group. What determines how many rows are written to a row group is complicated when there is no minimum, but in some circumstances, might lead to very small row groups. If you find that the Parquet files in your output datasets contain row groups that have a very small number of rows, try adjusting this setting. Note that changing this setting can result in a large increase in how much memory is used—Arrow already generally tries to write as large row groups as possible.

### 5.5.4.4 `max_partitions`

The maximum number of partitions any batch may be written into.

If you have a partitioning column that has an extremely large number of unique values, this setting is one you could consider changing. Note that if your partitioning column does have a large number of unique values, that is almost always a sign that you should not be partitioning by this variable. If you are tuning this option, you should first re-evaluate your partitioning strategy.

### 5.5.4.5 `max_open_files`

The maximum number of files that can be left opened during a write operation.

The more files we allow to be kept open at once, the less likely it is that Arrow will need to write multiple Parquet files per partition. However, keeping too many files open at once can lead to high memory consumption and other performance issues. This naturally creates a tension between minimizing the number of files that need to be written, and minimizing the amount of memory required for file writing.

Operating systems generally do not allow for a very large number of files to be open at once—common limits at the time of writing are between approximately 1024 and 4096. There are sometimes ways to raise this limit at the filesystem level, but these limits are there for a reason: they help the filesystem effectively interact with the underlying storage.

Arrow, by default, sets this to be slightly below the common lower bound for file limits. This way it generally works with most operating systems. In most circumstances, this should not be changed, but if you find yourself with a large number of small Parquet files in your partitions, increasing this number might help. Be sure, however, to consult with the operating system you're running on before increasing this. Exceeding their limit will cause issues, and circumventing their limits is almost always a mistake.

### 5.5.4.6 An example of tuning `max_rows_per_file`

We won't go into details about each of the possible settings above, but as an example, let's look at the maximum number of rows in each file. Let's say we want to restrict each file to contain 500,000 rows or fewer; to do this, we can pass in the `max_rows_per_file` parameter.

```
open_dataset("./data/person") |>
  filter(year >= 2018) |>
  group_by(year) |>
  write_dataset(
    file.path(tmp_dir, "person_starting_2018"),
    max_rows_per_file = 500000
  )
```

If we take a look at the files created, we now see there are seven in each of the year-partitioned directories.

```
fs::dir_ls(
  file.path(tmp_dir, "person_starting_2018"),
  recurse = TRUE
)
```

```
./data/transient_data/person_starting_2018/year=2018
./data/transient_data/person_starting_2018/year=2018/part-0.parquet
./data/transient_data/person_starting_2018/year=2018/part-1.parquet
./data/transient_data/person_starting_2018/year=2018/part-2.parquet
./data/transient_data/person_starting_2018/year=2018/part-3.parquet
./data/transient_data/person_starting_2018/year=2018/part-4.parquet
./data/transient_data/person_starting_2018/year=2018/part-5.parquet
./data/transient_data/person_starting_2018/year=2018/part-6.parquet
./data/transient_data/person_starting_2018/year=2019
./data/transient_data/person_starting_2018/year=2019/part-0.parquet
./data/transient_data/person_starting_2018/year=2019/part-1.parquet
./data/transient_data/person_starting_2018/year=2019/part-2.parquet
./data/transient_data/person_starting_2018/year=2019/part-3.parquet
./data/transient_data/person_starting_2018/year=2019/part-4.parquet
./data/transient_data/person_starting_2018/year=2019/part-5.parquet
./data/transient_data/person_starting_2018/year=2019/part-6.parquet
./data/transient_data/person_starting_2018/year=2021
./data/transient_data/person_starting_2018/year=2021/part-0.parquet
./data/transient_data/person_starting_2018/year=2021/part-1.parquet
./data/transient_data/person_starting_2018/year=2021/part-2.parquet
./data/transient_data/person_starting_2018/year=2021/part-3.parquet
./data/transient_data/person_starting_2018/year=2021/part-4.parquet
./data/transient_data/person_starting_2018/year=2021/part-5.parquet
./data/transient_data/person_starting_2018/year=2021/part-6.parquet
./data/transient_data/person_starting_2018/year=2022
./data/transient_data/person_starting_2018/year=2022/part-0.parquet
./data/transient_data/person_starting_2018/year=2022/part-1.parquet
./data/transient_data/person_starting_2018/year=2022/part-2.parquet
./data/transient_data/person_starting_2018/year=2022/part-3.parquet
./data/transient_data/person_starting_2018/year=2022/part-4.parquet
./data/transient_data/person_starting_2018/year=2022/part-5.parquet
./data/transient_data/person_starting_2018/year=2022/part-6.parquet
```

We can also see here that the default name for the file in each partition is `part-i.parquet` where i is the file number in that directory with values starting from 0.

To summarize, the following advice can be followed about partitioning your data:

- partition on the variables you filter on most often
- avoid ending up with partitions smaller than 20 MB or larger than 2 GB
- avoid ending up with a large number of files
- when in doubt, experiment with some queries which are typical of your usual workflow

There are extra considerations to pay attention to around partitioning if you are working with data in cloud storage; see Chapter 6 for more information on this.

## 5.6   Schemas

When you create an Arrow dataset, unless you supply the schema yourself, arrow will infer it automatically. In the case of formats like Parquet which include metadata about the column types, arrow's default behavior is to set the schema by reading in the first file in the dataset and using the information in its metadata to create the schema.

If you're working with a format which doesn't contain this additional metadata, such as CSV, arrow will read an initial block of data in the first file it scans, and infer the data type of each column based on the values it finds. The default block size when arrow reads CSV data is 1 MB—so the number or rows used to infer the schema will vary depending on the data in each column, total number of columns, and how many bytes each value takes up in memory. If all of the values in a column that lie within the first 1 MB of the file are missing values, arrow will classify this data as `null` type. Sparsely populated data, or variables that are not defined for a large enough subset of the data, can trigger this scenario. Generally, we recommend specifying a schema when working with CSV datasets to avoid potential issues like this. You can read more about type inference in Section 4.2.2.

Regardless of dataset format, leaving the default value of the parameter `unify_schemas` set to `FALSE` means that arrow will use the schema of the first file it encounters as the schema for the dataset. This works well when you can be confident that all of your files have the same, correct, schema. However, if not, we recommend that you either:

- manually specify the schema of the dataset, or
- tell arrow to scan all files in the dataset and combine their schemas with the argument `unify_schema = TRUE`

Use the second option when you are confident that the schemas for individual files are correct, but are not sure that each file in your dataset contains every possible column from the overall dataset. It can also be helpful as a check to confirm that the schemas of all of the files are compatible with each other. In other words: you don't have one column, split across multiple files, but containing different data types in different files, some of which are incompatible with each other.

### 5.6.1   Specifying a dataset schema

You can extract the schema of a dataset by calling the `schema()` function:

```
pums_person <- open_dataset("./data/person")
pums_schema <- schema(pums_person)
```

Let's say we wanted to update the schema of dataset. We could view the entire schema by inspecting the `pums_schema` object, or look at a single column like this:

```
pums_schema[["AGEP"]]
```

```
Field
AGEP: int32
```

Say we instead wanted this column representing age, instead of being a 32-bit integer, to be an 8-bit integer. Eight-bit integers have a maximum value of 127, which seems reasonable given the verified oldest person in the world was 122! We can update the value in the schema object by assigning the new type, and then re-opening the dataset with the updated schema.

```
pums_schema[["AGEP"]] <- int8()
pums_person_updated <- open_dataset("./data/person", schema = pums_schema)
```

We can then take a look at the type of the column in the updated version of the dataset, and we can see it is our new value.

```
schema(pums_person_updated)[["AGEP"]]
```

```
Field
AGEP: int8
```

For more on manipulating schemas, see Section 4.2.2.

### 5.6.2 Schemas from datasets with different columns in each file

If you are working with a directory of files in which some files have some columns missing, but you want your final dataset to contain every possible column, you can tell arrow to check the columns present in all files and then combine these to form the dataset schema.

```
open_dataset("./data/person", unify_schemas = TRUE)
```

Setting this option as `TRUE` may result in slower dataset initialization since arrow has to read the schema from every file in the dataset.

---

## 5.7 Sources

In the examples so far, we've showed creating datasets based on setting the `sources` argument to the parent path where the files in your dataset are stored, but you can also pass any of the following to `sources`:

- a path to a single file
- a list of files stored in multiple directories
- the URI of a directory on cloud storage, for example, an S3 bucket
- a list of dataset objects

### 5.7.1 Datasets consisting of individually-specified files

Generally, the simplest way to work with datasets is if all of the files that you want to be part of your dataset are in the same directory, but what if you want to include files from multiple locations? It is possible to work with files in multiple directories in arrow by passing in a list of files to `open_dataset()`.

```
ds <- open_dataset(
  sources = c(
    "./data/person/year=2021/location=ak/part-0.parquet",
    "./data/person/year=2021/location=wa/part-0.parquet"
  )
)
```

Although this will work, arrow will no longer automatically detect Hive partitions as variables in your dataset. This means that our `year` column will not be found:

```
pull(head(ds), "year")
```

```
Error in `pull()`:
! Can't extract columns that don't exist.
x Column `year` doesn't exist.
```

### 5.7.2   Excluding files based on filename or file validity

You may have extra files you want to store alongside your dataset files, but they aren't actually the row and column level data. For example, you might have a text file that includes a data dictionary in each folder next to each Parquet file in your dataset. You don't want to read in those text files when you are reading in the Parquet files.[3] You can specify extra options to `open_dataset()` to exclude these files from your dataset.

Let's say you have a directory containing your dataset, but also containing metadata in each subdirectory.

```
fs::dir_ls(file.path(tmp_dir, "person_with_metadata"), recurse = TRUE)
```

```
./data/transient_data/person_with_metadata/year=2019
./data/transient_data/person_with_metadata/year=2019/data_info.txt
./data/transient_data/person_with_metadata/year=2019/part-0.parquet
./data/transient_data/person_with_metadata/year=2021
./data/transient_data/person_with_metadata/year=2021/data_info.txt
./data/transient_data/person_with_metadata/year=2021/part-0.parquet
./data/transient_data/person_with_metadata/year=2022
./data/transient_data/person_with_metadata/year=2022/data_info.txt
./data/transient_data/person_with_metadata/year=2022/part-0.parquet
```

If you call `open_dataset()` on this directory, you'll get an error message as arrow will try (and fail) to read in the `data_info.txt` files as Parquet files.

```
open_dataset(file.path(tmp_dir, "person_with_metadata"))
```

```
Error in `open_dataset()`:
! Invalid: Error creating dataset. Could not read schema from
'./data/transient_data/person_with_metadata/year=2019/data_info.txt':
Parquet magic bytes not found in footer. Either the file is corrupted or
this is not a parquet file.
i Did you mean to specify a 'format' other than the default (parquet)?
```

However, you can set an option which tells arrow to ignore all files beginning with "data_".

```
open_dataset(
  file.path(tmp_dir, "person_with_metadata"),
  factory_options = list(selector_ignore_prefixes = c("data_"))
)
```

Alternatively, you can let arrow try to read in all the files, but exclude an invalid files.

---

[3]Also, where would that data go? The Parquet files already have the schema they need.

```
open_dataset(
  file.path(tmp_dir, "person_with_metadata"),
  factory_options = list(exclude_invalid_files = TRUE)
)
```

This approach may be slower than the previous one as arrow has to try to read in all of the files to see if they are valid, but can be useful when there is no common prefix to exclude files by.

### 5.7.3 Combining datasets

You may have datasets that consist of files in multiple formats. For example, perhaps you have a nightly ETL job that turns CSV to Parquet, but you want to analyze all of the data, including the newest CSV-only data that hasn't been converted to Parquet yet.

You still need to be able to work with the old data as well as the new data and analyze it together. In arrow it is possible to combine multiple datasets into a single dataset. First, we create a dataset from the Parquet data. In the example below, all we need to do is pass arrow the path to the Parquet dataset. The creation of the CSV dataset requires a bit more effort as we can't rely on the use of metadata to help us, like with the Parquet data. We need to pass `skip = 1` so the header row isn't read in as data, manually set the schema of the CSV data using the schema from the Parquet dataset, and also pass in another schema describing the partitioning variable. We can then use `dplyr::union_all()` to combine our two datasets into one.

```
parquet_dataset <- open_dataset(
  file.path(tmp_dir, "person_multiformat/parquet_data")
)
csv_dataset <- open_csv_dataset(
  file.path(tmp_dir, "person_multiformat/csv_data"),
  skip = 1,
  schema = schema(parquet_dataset),
  partitioning = schema(year = int32(), location = string())
)
```

```
combined_data <- dplyr::union_all(csv_dataset, parquet_dataset)
```

We can now query this dataset as if it was a single dataset.

```
combined_data |>
  group_by(year) |>
  summarise(
    mean_age = sum(JWMNP * PWGTP, na.rm = TRUE) / sum(PWGTP)
  ) |>
  collect()
```

```
# A tibble: 2 x 2
   year mean_age
  <int>    <dbl>
1  2021     9.78
2  2018    12.1
```

## 5.8   Summary

In this chapter, we looked at working with Arrow Datasets to work with larger-than-memory data. We discussed how partitioning data based on columns in the dataset allows us to store the data across multiple files and directories. We saw that the simplest strategy for deciding how to partition your data is to choose columns that you often filter your data on, but ultimately, it's worth experimenting with your own data and seeing what works best for your particular workflow. We saw at how schema inference works with Parquet and CSV files, as well as how to create datasets consisting of files from multiple sources.

# 6

## *Cloud*

In the previous chapters, we've discussed working with data which is stored on a local filesystem, but Arrow also can also work with data stored on a remote machine.

If you want to read a single file directly into memory, you can pass a URL directly into a file-reading function, and the file will be downloaded to a temporary directory and then loaded into your R session.

```
read_parquet(
  "https://github.com/apache/arrow/raw/main/r/inst/v0.7.1.parquet"
)
```

```
# A tibble: 10 x 11
   carat cut    color clarity depth table price     x     y     z
   <dbl> <chr>  <chr> <chr>   <dbl> <dbl> <int> <dbl> <dbl> <dbl>
 1  0.23 Ideal  E     SI2      61.5    55   326  3.95  3.98  2.43
 2  0.21 Prem~  E     SI1      59.8    61   326  3.89  3.84  2.31
 3  0.23 Good   E     VS1      56.9    65   327  4.05  4.07  2.31
 4  0.29 Prem~  I     VS2      62.4    58   334  4.2   4.23  2.63
 5  0.31 Good   J     SI2      63.3    58   335  4.34  4.35  2.75
 6  0.24 Very~  J     VVS2     62.8    57   336  3.94  3.96  2.48
 7  0.24 Very~  I     VVS1     62.3    57   336  3.95  3.98  2.47
 8  0.26 Very~  H     SI1      61.9    55   337  4.07  4.11  2.53
 9  0.22 Fair   E     VS2      65.1    61   337  3.87  3.78  2.49
10  0.23 Very~  H     VS1      59.4    61   338  4     4.05  2.39
# i 1 more variable: `__index_level_0__` <int>
```

If you want to work with multi-file datasets, however, the HTTP protocol isn't compatible with Arrow's ability to scan files and read metadata before data is accessed to optimize what is eventually pulled into memory upon collecting a query. Working with multi-file datasets is possible though when accessing remote data kept in cloud storage services such as Amazon Simple Storage Service (S3) and Google Cloud Storage (GCS).

There are different reasons that you might be working with cloud data, for example:

- datasets which are too large to be stored on a local machine
- datasets being accessed as part of a process rather than interactively, e.g. data for a Shiny app deployed online
- datasets which belong to someone else that you have been granted access to or using open data hosted on cloud filesystems

In these circumstances, storing data in the cloud can offer multiple benefits:

- infrastructure can be scaled easily as the data grows

- using a managed environment can increase reliability and uptime, and lower the need for maintenance
- access can be provided to people in different locations easily

However, there are some challenges which come with this, in terms of data storage and retrieval costs, as well as the potential for slow transfer times, which becomes increasing likely with larger workloads.

If the data is static (i.e. not being updated) and of a reasonable size to store on disk, then a relatively simple workflow would be to download the entire dataset and run calculations on it locally. This isn't always feasible if the dataset is too large or if the data transfer time would negatively impact performance, and so an alternative is needed.

Fortunately, Arrow can help. Since storing data in Parquet format uses much less space than the equivalent CSV file, using Arrow can reduce both data storage and transfer costs. On top of that, transfer costs can also be further reduced by taking advantage of Arrow's use of partitioning, only transferring the minimum data required from cloud storage to complete the query.

In this chapter, we'll take a look at how to work with data which is hosted on cloud platforms, outline some platform-specific considerations, and show you how to work the most efficiently with cloud data.

While we focus on Parquet datasets, the techniques shown here can be used on CSV datasets. CSVs work fine, but they're slower and more expensive. While you can work with compressed CVSs, this solves part of the problem, but not all of it[1].

Many examples will look at working with data hosted on Amazon S3, but the same principles can also be used with data in GCS. There are some subtle differences between S3 and GCS which we'll highlight when they come up and outline any differences you need to be aware of. In the future, the Apache Arrow project plans to add functionality to work with additional cloud storage services like Azure Blob Storage—this implementation and future ones relating to any other cloud storage services will also follow this model.[2]

In cloud storage terminology, S3 and GCS refer to the place where the data is stored as a **bucket**. Other systems may use alternative terms, like "blob", but we will use "bucket" here as a generic term.

---

## 6.1   Working with data in cloud storage

Working with cloud storage services is similar in many ways to working with data stored in local filesystems, and you can use the same file and dataset opening functions for both tasks. To open a file or dataset saved in cloud storage, instead of passing in a path to a local file to these functions, you can instead pass in the cloud storage path as a URI.

```
read_parquet(
  paste0(
```

---

[1] The lack of metadata with this format reduces the number of optimizations that Arrow can take advantage of. You can read more about working with compressed CSVs in Section 4.2.3.

[2] At the time of writing, the Arrow C++ library has introduced support for Azure Blob Storage. Users of PyArrow can query datasets on Azure from Python, and once bindings are added to the arrow R package, it will be available from R.

```
    "s3://scaling-arrow-pums/person/year=2005/",
    "location=ak/part-0.parquet"
  )
)
open_dataset("s3://scaling-arrow-pums/person/")
```

Note that when working with data stored on GCS, even when working with a publicly accessible bucket, you'll need to provide a login name of "anonymous". The equivalent of the above commands for GCS—these won't run here as these buckets haven't been set up—would be:

```
read_parquet(
  paste0(
    "gs://anonymous@scaling-arrow-pums/person/year=2005/",
    "location=ak/part-0.parquet"
  )
)
open_dataset("gs://anonymous@scaling-arrow-pums/person/")
```

Now let's take a closer look at running queries in the cloud. If we create a new dataset connecting to the S3 bucket and take a look at the object, we'll see it looks the same as a local dataset.

```
person_data <- open_dataset("s3://scaling-arrow-pums/person/")
person_data
```

```
FileSystemDataset with 884 Parquet files
311 columns
SPORDER: int32
RT: dictionary<values=string, indices=int32>
SERIALNO: string
PUMA: string
ST: string
ADJUST: int32
PWGTP: int32
AGEP: int32
CIT: dictionary<values=string, indices=int32>
COW: dictionary<values=string, indices=int32>
DDRS: bool
DEYE: bool
DOUT: bool
DPHY: bool
DREM: bool
DWRK: bool
ENG: dictionary<values=string, indices=int32>
FER: bool
GCL: bool
GCM: dictionary<values=string, indices=int32>
...
291 more columns
Use `schema()` to see entire schema
```

The key difference here is that we know that the data is stored on the cloud. One of the advantages of working with arrow when dealing with cloud datasets is that we can take advantage of both partitioning and lazy evaluation—we can construct the query that we're going to run on our dataset without pulling anything into memory or transferring the data from cloud storage to our local machine.

Let's write a query which will calculate the highest age recorded in the dataset for the state of California in 2022.

```
max_age_ca_2022 <- person_data |>
  filter(year == 2022, location == "ca") |>
  summarize(max_age = max(AGEP))

max_age_ca_2022

FileSystemDataset (query)
max_age: int32

See $.data for the source Arrow object
```

Again, it looks just like the same query would when set up to run on a local copy of the data. Now when we call `collect()` to pull the data into our R session, we will only download a subset of the data necessary to run our query.

```
collect(max_age_ca_2022)

# A tibble: 1 x 1
  max_age
    <int>
1      94
```

An important question to ask here is how long it took to run the query. We compared running the same query from above on the same machine—a Posit Cloud instance with 1 GB of RAM—with a local copy of the data compared to the cloud version of the same data. The results are shown in Table 6.1.

Table 6.1: Time taken to run the same query on a local machine and connecting to an S3 bucket

| Location | Time (s) |
|----------|----------|
| Local    | 0.2      |
| Cloud    | 24.1     |

There's a huge difference between these results: it was 120 times faster to work with a local copy of the data! This was due to the need for data transfer; in the local query, Arrow could just scan the data and perform the necessary calculations, whereas in the cloud query, we needed to download the data first before we could return it to our R session.

A reasonable question to ask here might be why did it took 24 seconds to run a query which only had one row of data in the results? The answer to this question is that we actually downloaded more than one row of data—in fact, we downloaded all of the data for California in 2022—with the final aggregation being performed locally. Let's take a look at the reasons for this, and see what we can do to minimize data transfer in our queries.

## 6.2 Working efficiently with cloud data

Pulling data from cloud storage can be slow—the main bottleneck is transferring data over the internet—and it takes longer than querying data locally. Given that increased data transfer results in increased costs and slower retrieval of results, it's important to understand how to minimize the amount of data that needs to be downloaded.

### 6.2.1 Minimizing data transfer

In this section, we'll look at how we can run queries on the cloud datasets but only download a relevant subset of the data, and discuss different strategies for minimizing data transfer when working with data in cloud storage.

Tools for measuring data transfer vary between different operating systems; in the code examples below, we'll show the output from a Linux tool called nethogs[3]. If you want to test out data transfer yourself, see Section A.3.1 for more information about the commands we ran to measure bandwidth.

#### 6.2.1.1 Partitioning

We introduced strategies for efficient partitioning when working with datasets in Chapter 5, but this becomes even more important when working with data in cloud storage.

The full copy of the PUMS person dataset is just under 8 GB of Parquet files. Let's say we want to collect a subset of the PUMS person dataset, filtering to include only data from respondents in California in 2022. Let's take a look at our local copy to see how many rows of data this is.

```
open_dataset("./data/person") |>
  filter(year == 2022, location == "ca") |>
  nrow()
```

```
[1] 391171
```

The resulting dataset contains just under 400,000 rows of data, which takes up just under 60 MB on disk.

The crucial question we want to ask next is: how much data is transferred to our local machine when run the same query on the dataset stored in S3 and then retrieve the results? Let's run the code to get the data:

```
ca_2022 <- open_dataset("s3://scaling-arrow-pums/person") |>
  filter(year == 2022, location == "ca") |>
  collect()
```

Running that query downloaded 61.8 MB of data, closely matching the amount of space that the Parquet files in the dataset take up on disk. It's slightly higher by a couple of megabytes, but this is due to other transfer overhead, such as connecting to the S3 bucket itself and reading the file headers.

---

[3]https://github.com/raboof/nethogs

Now, what if we want to filter to only return data for individuals who are the maximum age we found earlier— 94? Let's count the rows of data.

```
open_dataset("s3://scaling-arrow-pums/person") |>
  filter(year == 2022, location == "ca", AGEP == 94) |>
  nrow()
```

```
[1] 3111
```

This is a much smaller subset—around 3,000 rows of data compared to 400,000. So how much data is transferred when we run this on S3?

```
ca_2022_94 <- open_dataset("s3://scaling-arrow-pums/person") |>
  filter(year == 2022, location == "ca", AGEP == 94) |>
  collect()
```

The amount of data transferred was 61.8 MB, exactly the same as last time—so what's going on here?

Arrow is able to use the partition variables `year` and `location` to work out which files contain the data needed, in both examples. In the second example, arrow needs access to the values in the files to be able to filter by `AGEP` and so all values in the files have to be transferred first. In this dataset, there is one file per unique combination of `year` and `location` and so we know the data we need must be in a single file. If the data is split across multiple files, arrow can make use of the Parquet file metadata—more on that later—to work out whether that file needs downloading.

This shows the need for careful thought when deciding how to partition your data that you'll be keeping in cloud storage—you can reduce transfer costs significantly by partitioning data on columns which are more commonly used in filters. This must, however, be balanced with not creating too many partitions, otherwise transfers may be slowed down significantly by the need to access large numbers of individual files.

As with the examples we discussed in Chapter 5, when deciding how to partition your data, experimentation can help in working out how to strike the right balance.

While partitioning can help reduce the total amount of data transferred when working with any arrow-compatible formats in cloud storage, working specifically with Parquet files brings some additional advantages, which we'll take a look at in the next section.

### 6.2.1.2 Parquet statistics

Another way in which arrow can limit the amount of data transferred over the network is taking advantage of statistics stored in Parquet metadata.

Let's say we wanted to take the entire dataset and retrieve a subset which only includes people aged 97 or older, across all years and locations. We can run the following query.

```
open_dataset("s3://scaling-arrow-pums/person/") |>
  filter(AGEP >= 97) |>
  write_dataset("./data/transient_data/olds")
```

The resulting file was 228 KB in total, with 110 MB of data transferred even though the query itself is not limited to our specific partitioning columns: `year` or `location`.

So how is it possible that we only downloaded a subset of the full dataset despite filtering on a non-partitioning column? And why did it require 110 MB of data to be transferred?

Parquet metadata contains information about minimum and maximum values in each of the columns in each file. This means that arrow can inspect this metadata and only return data from files which might contain relevant values, filtering this data further locally once it's been downloaded from cloud storage.

If we take a look at our local copy of the data, we can apply the same filter, extract the names of the files from which the filtered rows appear in, and then look at their total size.

```
open_dataset("data/person/") |>
  filter(AGEP >= 97) |>
  transmute(filename = add_filename()) |>
  distinct() |>
  pull(as_vector = TRUE) |>
  map_int(fs::file_size) |>
  sum() |>
  fs::as_fs_bytes()
```

4.88M

This is still way less than the 110 MB of data transferred, so how do we account for the additional 105 MB?

The problem here is that we haven't accounted for the data transferred when arrow reads the file headers so it can use the statistics to work out whether the file contains relevant data to filter further locally.

To find out how much data is transferred to inspect the headers, we can take a baseline measure that looks at how much data is transferred if we run a query that results in 0 rows of data being saved to disk. We can filter the dataset to only include respondents with an age greater than 1097 years.

```
open_dataset("s3://scaling-arrow-pums/person/") |>
  filter(AGEP >= 1097) |>
  write_dataset("./data/transient_data/ancients")
```

Nothing was written to disk as the resulting dataset contained 0 rows, but 105 MB of data was transferred. Those 105 MB of data are our Parquet file headers; when we add that to the total sizes of the files containing relevant data, 5 MB, we get the total amount of data transferred: 110 MB.

The same principle can also be applied to missing values If your data has a lot of missing values, Parquet statistics contain metadata about how many values in each column are missing, so arrow can skip transferring files when there is no data present in a column.

### 6.2.2   Network location and transfer speed

Another consideration when working with cloud data like this is the relative geographic locations of where the data is stored, and the location of the computer which is accessing the data.

### 6.2.2.1   Selecting a bucket region

If you're setting up a new cloud storage bucket, you'll see faster performance when query-ing data if you choose a region which is geographically close to the machines from which individual users or apps will be accessing the data from, and even faster performance when within the same network.

To demonstrate this, we took a look at the speed of running a query which returned the data for California in 2022.

```
tf <- tempfile()
dir.create(tf)
open_dataset("s3://scaling-arrow-pums/person") |>
  filter(year == 2022, location == "ca") |>
  write_dataset(tf)
```

The resulting file was a 60 MB Parquet file.

We ran this query on Nic's laptop connecting to the following buckets:

1. the original S3 bucket located in `us-east-1` region
2. an identical bucket located in the `eu-west-2` region, in London

We then tried the queried the original S3 bucket again, but from a Posit Cloud instance deployed on Amazon EC2 in the `us-east-1` region.

The average times across 3 runs are shown in Table 6.2.

Table 6.2: Time taken to run the same query with varying bucket location and access location

| Bucket location | Access location | Time (seconds) |
|---|---|---|
| Virginia, US (us-east-1) | Manchester, UK | 56 |
| London, UK (eu-west-2) | Manchester, UK | 50 |
| Virginia, US (us-east-1) | Virginia, US (us-east-1) | 24 |

Using a bucket in the same geographical region resulted in a slight decrease in time to run the query and collect the data, when transferring the results to work with locally. However, geographic location alone wasn't the sole factor determining transfer times.

The time to complete the query was significantly shorter on Posit Cloud deployed on EC2 than when transferring to a machine outside of the AWS network. The speed up is because of the interconnection between AWS data centers as well as the fact that the data is now being transferred within AWS's internal network with optimized infrastructure, rather than over the internet.

It's also worth keeping in mind the impact on cost—not just in terms of speed, but money too. At time of writing, it was free to transfer data from an S3 bucket to another AWS service like EC2 within the same AWS region, but there were charges associated with transferring data between regions, or out to the internet, which was the most expensive of all.

## 6.3 Working directly with a bucket object

The previous examples in this chapter all involved working with datasets by passing in a URI. This is the simplest path to working with data in cloud storage, though you might need a finer degree of control to go beyond the default configuration. In such cases, you can work directly with a bucket object.

You can create an object representing the connection to the bucket itself, which can then be manipulated further, allowing the possibility of passing in additional parameters, such as those relating to authentication.

```
bucket <- s3_bucket("scaling-arrow-pums")
```

Now that we're connected to the bucket, let's take a look around. We can use the `ls()` method to list all the directories inside the bucket.

```
bucket$ls()
```

```
[1] "household"   "person"      "raw_csvs"     "readme.html"
```

If we want to look further into an individual directory, we can pass in the name of the directory to `ls()` to take a look inside. Let's check out the contents of the **person** directory.

```
bucket$ls("person")
```

```
 [1] "person/year=2005" "person/year=2006" "person/year=2007"
 "person/year=2008" "person/year=2009" "person/year=2010"
 "person/year=2011"
 [8] "person/year=2012" "person/year=2013" "person/year=2014"
 "person/year=2015" "person/year=2016" "person/year=2017"
 "person/year=2018"
[15] "person/year=2019" "person/year=2021" "person/year=2022"
```

If we want to work just with the data in this directory, we can use the `path()` method to create a new object that points just to this directory, e.g.

```
person_bucket <- bucket$path("person")
```

And what if we want to list all of the files inside our bucket? We can pass the argument `recursive = TRUE` to the `ls()` method. Let's take a look at the first 10 elements of the contents of the 2022 directory.

```
person_2022_data <- person_bucket$path("year=2022")
head(person_2022_data$ls(recursive = TRUE), n = 10)
```

```
 [1] "location=ak/part-0.parquet" "location=ak"
 "location=al/part-0.parquet" "location=al"
 [5] "location=ar/part-0.parquet" "location=ar"
 "location=az/part-0.parquet" "location=az"
 [9] "location=ca/part-0.parquet" "location=ca"
```

Just as if we wanted to list all of the files in the local copy by calling `fs::dir_ls("./data/person/year=2022")`, we can see that the call to the `ls()` method above lists both the directories and files stored inside of them. In S3, this is the default, but if working with GCS, you must pass in the argument `recursive = TRUE` to get all of the files and directories.

Now we've connected to the bucket, how do we actually work with the data? As mentioned earlier in this chapter, the simplest way, if you have a single file which you want to read entirely into memory is using the same `read_*` functions you'd use to work with a local file, passing in the path to the file or dataset on cloud storage.

If you've created a bucket object, this can also be passed into `read_parquet()` and other file-reading functions or `open_dataset()`.

```
person_data <- open_dataset(person_bucket)
```

The examples we've looked at so far have all been on a bucket that hasn't required us to provide any login details, but what about if we want to connect to a bucket which requires us to provide credentials? We'll take a look at that in the next section.

## 6.4   Authentication

There are multiple options for how provide credential when connecting to S3 or GCS, and these methods of authentication vary between providers.

In this section, we're going to talk about:

- anonymous login
- passing credentials in manually
- using a credentials file
- using environment variables

Different methods of authentication are more suitable for different circumstances. In short:

- anonymous login is fine for accessing publicly-accessible buckets but won't work for private buckets where you need to supply credentials
- the simplest method is to pass in your credentials manually as parameters, but it is also the least secure
- passing in credentials via an environment variable is great for when you are using a script and don't want the details hard-coded where other people can see them
- using a credentials file removes the need to manually pass in credentials once it's been configured

If you already have been working with cloud storage services via another program or the command line, you might already have one of these options configured. It's important to only use one method to prevent confusion if the values are in conflict.

There are other possible methods, which you can find more information about in the AWS docs[4] or the GCS docs[5]. We've included some examples of the most common methods below. At the time of writing these are how the methods work, but this might change. As always, look to the relevant docs for the most up-to-date methods and best practices.

---

[4] https://docs.aws.amazon.com/sdk-for-cpp/v1/developer-guide/credentials.html
[5] https://cloud.google.com/docs/authentication

Generally, we recommend using a credentials file when working locally, but environment variables when working with applications deployed online.

In the next section, we'll walk through the different options.

### 6.4.1 Anonymous

If you're connecting to a publicly accessible bucket, you can log in anonymously, but how you do this differs between S3 and AWS.

#### 6.4.1.1 S3

If you're connecting to a public S3 bucket, you don't need to pass in any credentials.

```
bucket <- s3_bucket("scaling-arrow-pums")
```

However, if you already have AWS credentials configured via another method, such as a credentials file, you should pass in the `anonymous = TRUE` argument to prevent those credentials being automatically detected and used, otherwise access may fail.

```
bucket <- s3_bucket("scaling-arrow-pums", anonymous = TRUE)
```

#### 6.4.1.2 GCS

In GCS, different host names are used depending on whether the user is logged in or not. This means that if you want to connect to a GCS instance without providing authentication credentials, you must manually set `anonymous` to `TRUE` to make sure that the correct host name is used.

```
bucket <- gs_bucket(
  "scaling-arrow-pums/person/",
  anonymous = TRUE
)
```

### 6.4.2 Manually pass in credentials

The simplest way to connect to a private bucket is to pass in credentials manually. These methods are fine for working with code interactively, but run the risk of accidentally being checked into version control and exposing these details to others. This isn't arrow-specific advice, but rather, is general best practice. Putting secrets in your code means they're in your command history, as well as possibly checked into source control and exposed.

#### 6.4.2.1 S3

In AWS S3, this is done using your login, `access_key` and password, `secret_key` into `s3_bucket()` when creating a new connection.

```
secret_data <- s3_bucket(
  "secret_bucket_name",
  access_key = "nic",
  secret_key = "12345"
)
```

Similarly, you can pass all of these details in as a single URI string.

```
secret_data <- s3_bucket("s3://nic:12345@secret_bucket_name")
```

#### 6.4.2.2 GCS

In GCS, you'll need to get an access token and its expiration date, which you can then pass into the call to `gs_bucket()`.

```
secret_data <- gs_bucket(
  "secret_bucket_name",
  access_token = "ab12.ABCS6ZRVmB7fkLtd1XTmq6mo0s-6Uw7p8vtgSwg",
  expiration = as.POSIXct("2024-08-09 12:00:00")
)
```

### 6.4.3  A credentials file

Credentials files can be a convenient way of configuring your authentication and other configuration without having to manually set multiple environment variables.

#### 6.4.3.1  S3

AWS credentials files can be a convenient way of configuring your authentication and other configuration without having to manually set multiple environment variables. AWS credentials files are typically stored for Linux and macOS users at `~/.aws/credentials` or `C:\Users\<username>\.aws\credentials` for Windows users, though you can store them in another location and set the `AWS_SHARED_CREDENTIALS_FILE` environment variable to point to their location to ensure they are automatically detected.

When the AWS SDK is initialized, it will look for this credentials file automatically, so you don't need to make any changes in your code in order to be able to use them.

#### 6.4.3.2  GCS

If you need to provide credentials, and have the Google Cloud CLI installed, you can set up a local credentials file by setting up Application Default Credential (ADC) by running the following code from the command line:

```
gcloud auth application-default login
```

### 6.4.4  Environment variables

A more secure method of authentication when working with cloud storage in applications deployed on continuous integration (CI) systems like GitHub Actions is the use of environment variables. Using this method means that the credentials don't appear in your code or console logs anywhere, and thus can be a useful of ensuring your credentials remain secure if you want to share your code with others. By setting the environment variables outside of your script, you can share your code without sharing your credentials.

#### 6.4.4.1  S3

You can set the environment variables `AWS_ACCESS_KEY_ID` and `AWS_SECRET_ACCESS_KEY` to your access key and secret key, and the AWS SDK will automatically check if these variables have been set, and if they are, use the values in them to authenticate.

### 6.4.4.2 GCS

It's a little different with GCS: if deploying an application to a CI/CD system such as GitHub Actions, the `GOOGLE_APPLICATION_CREDENTIALS` environment variable should be pointed to the location of the JSON credentials file. As it wouldn't be secure to store this file in your repository, you'll need to take an alternative approach such as encoding your service account key and storing this value as another environment variable, decoding it within the CI, and then setting the `GOOGLE_APPLICATION_CREDENTIALS` variable to this location. The details of how to do this are beyond the scope of this book, but check out the Google Cloud documentation[6] for more information.

## 6.5  Configuring bucket region

If you don't specify the region that the data is stored in, then Arrow will work it out based on your configuration and a few different heuristics.

Providing this manually will speed up the initial bucket connection, though won't have an effect on subsequent analyses.

```
bucket <- s3_bucket("scaling-arrow-pums", region = "us-east-1")
bucket <- gs_bucket("scaling-arrow-pums", region = "US-EAST1")
```

## 6.6  Enabling Logging in S3

When working specifically data stored in AWS S3, arrow provides an interface to official libraries supplied by AWS, which are capable of detailed logging. By default, the AWS logging level is set to `FATAL`, meaning only critical errors that cause the code to fail will be shown.

However, if things aren't working as expected, you may want to select a different logging level to get a better idea of exactly what's going on. You can do this by setting the `ARROW_S3_LOG_LEVEL` environment variable.

```
Sys.setenv("ARROW_S3_LOG_LEVEL" = "DEBUG")
```

To manually set the logging level, you need to do this before you use any S3-related functions. If you need to change it later, you'll need to restart your R session first. This environment variable is read the first time during your R session that you use a function in arrow which uses the AWS SDK, initializing the SDK with settings which persist for the whole session.

The possible log levels, from least verbose to most verbose are: `"OFF"`, `"FATAL"` (the default), `"ERROR"`, `"WARN"`, `"INFO"`, `"DEBUG"`, and `"TRACE"`.

While the default logging level is usually sufficient, if you encounter issues like a slow connection or credentials not working, increasing the logging level can help you diagnose the problem.

---

[6]https://cloud.google.com/docs/authentication/provide-credentials-adc#local-key

## 6.7  Summary

In this chapter, we looked at working with data in cloud storage using arrow, including reading files from S3 and GCS, strategies for working efficiently with cloud data, including partitioning data effectively so that arrow can entirely skip scanning files which aren't relevant to the current query. We also saw how working with Parquet files enables arrow to use metadata in file headers to decide whether to download an individual file or not when executing a query. Additionally, we highlighted the importance of considering where the data is being accessed from, and configuring regions to optimize performance and reduce data transfer times. Finally, we covered working with bucket objects, and authentication.

Generally, if you're regularly analyzing data stored on S3 with arrow and looking to minimize data transfer costs, it's worth experimenting with dataset configuration to find the most efficient setup for your particular analysis needs.

This chapter provided an overview of the key practical steps and considerations for integrating cloud storage into your data workflows using Arrow. For more advanced functionality and detailed options, refer to the documentation for the `FileSystem`[7] classes.

---

[7]https://arrow.apache.org/docs/r/reference/FileSystem.html

# 7

## Advanced Topics

In this chapter we're going to dive into some more advanced topics. As we've shown in the previous chapters, the arrow R package includes support for hundreds of functions in R and has a rich type system. These empower you to solve most common data analysis problems. However, if you ever need to extend that set of functionalities, there are several options.

To start, we'll look in more detail at how bindings from R functions to Acero, the Arrow C++ query engine, work. We'll also explore the converse of this: functions that exist in Acero and don't have R equivalents, and how you can access these in your arrow pipelines. Then, we're going to show how you can call back from Acero into R to do calculations where functions you want to use inside don't have a corresponding Acero function. For other cases, we'll show how the Arrow format's focus on interoperability lets you stream data to and from other query engines, such as DuckDB, to access different functionality they have. Finally, we'll look at a practical case of extending Arrow's type system to work with geospatial data.

## 7.1 Acero

Acero is the Arrow C++ library's query execution engine. A query execution engine is a library which allows users to perform queries against a data source. It takes input data and the operations to be performed on the data, combines them, and returns the output from this process.

It typically has multiple steps, which could include things like:

- taking the query and parsing it into an algebraic format
- re-ordering and optimizing the query in order to run it in the most efficient way[1]
- actually running the query

When you call dplyr functions on Arrow tabular objects like tables and datasets, the code in the R package translates this into execution plan—directed graphs that express what operations need to take place. These operations are represented by nodes. For example, a `ProjectNode` is used to create a new column.

You can see the execution plan by running `show_query()`, which displays the execution plan, as a final step in a query.

---

[1] Acero doesn't have a logical query optimizer, but as we have seen, it does support optimizations like "predicate pushdown"—filtering the data where it is stored rather than in memory, which is what makes filtering on partitioned datasets fast. To take advantage of these optimizations, there is code in the R package that reorders queries before passing it to Acero for most common workflows.

DOI: 10.1201/9781032663197-7

```
open_dataset("data/person/") |>
  transmute(age_renamed = AGEP) |>
  show_query()
```

```
ExecPlan with 3 nodes:
2:SinkNode{}
  1:ProjectNode{projection=["age_renamed": AGEP]}
    0:SourceNode{}
```

In the example above, the `SourceNode` and the `SinkNode` provide the input and the output. The middle step, the `ProjectNode` is where the new column is created.

A more complex query will end up with more nodes representing the different operations.

```
open_dataset("data/person/") |>
  filter(location == "wa") |>
  group_by(year) |>
  summarize(mean_age = mean(AGEP)) |>
  show_query()
```

```
ExecPlan with 5 nodes:
4:SinkNode{}
  3:GroupByNode{keys=["year"], aggregates=[
    hash_mean(mean_age, {skip_nulls=false, min_count=0}),
  ]}
    2:ProjectNode{projection=["mean_age": AGEP, year]}
      1:FilterNode{filter=(location == "wa")}
        0:SourceNode{}
```

Generally, we don't have to worry about the details of these query plans, though they can be useful to get a closer look at exactly what is being run in Acero.

---

## 7.2   Acero function bindings

In Chapter 3, we mentioned that the arrow R package transforms dplyr syntax into Arrow Expressions which can be understood by Acero, and here we're going to dive into that a little deeper.

Acero has a large number of functions implemented for performing calculations and transformations on data. The complete list can be found in the project documentation[2].

Some of these functions have the same names are the R equivalent. For example, both Acero and R have a `min()` function which can be used to find the lowest value in a vector or array of values. Other functions have slightly different names. While in R we use the − operator to subtract one value from another, in Acero, there are functions `subtract()` and `subtract_checked()`. The latter function is more commonly used as it accounts for overflow[3] and raises an error if the value returned is beyond the minimum or maximum

---

[2]https://arrow.apache.org/docs/cpp/compute.html#available-functions

[3]Overflow is when a numeric value is larger than the type can support. For example, unsigned 8-bit integers can represent numbers 0-255. So if we add 250 + 10 we would have a value that is 260, which is not able to be represented with 8 bits. The checked variants of arithmetic calculations will raise an error in this case, which is almost always what we want in these circumstances.

value for that data type.

Let's take a closer look at an example.

## 7.2.1 A simple Acero binding

The query below calculates a new column, the age of the respondents in the previous year, by deducting 1 from the value in the `AGEP` column. There is already a mapping between the `-` operator in R and `subtract_checked()` in Acero, and we can see this by creating our query but not actually executing it.

```
open_dataset("data/person/") |>
  transmute(age_previous_year = AGEP - 1)
```

```
FileSystemDataset (query)
age_previous_year: int32 (subtract_checked(AGEP, 1))
```

```
See $.data for the source Arrow object
```

When we print the query, the output shows that new column `age_previous_year` is calculated by calling the Acero function `subtract_checked()` and passing in a reference to the `AGEP` column and the number `1`.

## 7.2.2 Bindings for more complex functions

Mappings also exist for slightly more complex functions that have additional parameters.

Say we wanted to only return data for states whose names start with the letter "w". We can take our dataset and use `dplyr::filter()` to return this subset, but we need to pick a function to pass to `dplyr::filter()` to actually *do* the filtering.

Let's start first by looking at the Acero function we want Arrow to use. To be clear: we wouldn't usually have to do this when working with arrow. This is just to illustrate how this all works.

If we look at the Acero compute function docs[4], we'll see that there is a function `starts_with` which does this. It has 2 options: `pattern`, the substring to match at the start of the string, and `ignore_case`, whether the matching should be case sensitive.

So how do we use this from the arrow R package? We start off by considering which R function to use. Let's go with the base R function `startsWith()`. Table 7.1 shows a comparison with the Acero equivalent.

Table 7.1: Comparing R's `sd` with Acero's `stddev`

|       | Function name | Function arguments | Prefix/Pattern argument | Case sensitivity |
|-------|---------------|--------------------|-------------------------|------------------|
| R     | startsWith    | prefix             | prefix: The prefix to match | Always case-sensitive |
| Acero | starts_with   | pattern, ignore_case | pattern: The pattern to match | ignore_case: Boolean, set to false by default |

---

[4]https://arrow.apache.org/docs/cpp/compute.html#available-functions

```
open_dataset("data/person/") |>
  select(location) |>
  filter(startsWith(x = location, prefix = "w"))
```

```
FileSystemDataset (query)
location: string
```

```
* Filter: starts_with(location, {pattern="w", ignore_case=false})
See $.data for the source Arrow object
```

The information about the Acero mapping is shown here in the line which starts with "*Filter". This contains a human-readable representation of the Arrow Expression created.

It shows that `startsWith()` has been translated to the Acero function `starts_with()`. The options for the Acero function have been set based on the values which were passed in via the R expression. We set the `startsWith()` argument `prefix` to "w", and that was passed to the Acero `starts_with()` option called `pattern`. As `startsWith()` is always case-sensitive, the Acero `starts_with()` option `ignore_case` has been set to `false`.

### 7.2.3 Bindings for aggregation functions

The arrow R package also has bindings for aggregation functions which take multiple rows of data and calculate a single value. For example, whereas R has `sd()` for calculating the standard deviation of a vector, Acero has `stddev()`.

Table 7.2: Comparing R's `sd` with Acero's `stddev`

|        | Function name | Function options | Handling of missing values | Degrees of freedom | Minimum count |
|--------|---------------|------------------|----------------------------|--------------------|---------------|
| R      | sd            | na.rm            | na.rm: Boolean, removes NA values (default FALSE) | Not implemented | Not implemented |
| Acero  | stddev        | ddof, skip_nulls, min_count | skip_nulls: Boolean, removes NULL values (default FALSE) | ddof: Integer, denominator degrees of freedom (default 0) | min_count: Integer, returns NULL if fewer non-null values are present (default 1) |

There are also some differences in the options for these functions; while R's `sd` function has arguments `x`, the value to be passed in and `na.rm`, whether to remove NA values or not, Acero's stddev also has `ddof`—denominator degrees of freedom, `skip_nulls`, the equivalent of `na_rm`, and `min_count`—if there are fewer values than this, return NULL.

```
open_dataset("data/person/") |>
  summarise(sd_age = sd(AGEP))
```

```
FileSystemDataset (query)
sd_age: double
```

See $.data for the source Arrow object

The output here doesn't show the function mapping as aggregation functions are handled differently from `select()`, `filter()`, and `mutate()`. The aggregation step is contained in the nested `.data` attribute of the query. This nesting ensures that the steps of the query are evaluated in this order. While `select()`, `filter()`, and `mutate()` can happen successively and be reflected in a single query step, any actions that happen on the data after `summarize()` (and, for that matter, joins) cannot be collapsed or rearranged like that.

You can see the full query by calling `show_query()` as a final step.

```
open_dataset("data/person/") |>
  summarise(sd_age = sd(AGEP)) |>
  show_query()
```

```
ExecPlan with 4 nodes:
3:SinkNode{}
  2:ScalarAggregateNode{aggregates=[
    stddev(sd_age, {ddof=1, skip_nulls=false, min_count=0}),
]}
    1:ProjectNode{projection=["sd_age": AGEP]}
      0:SourceNode{}
```

We can see in the output above a reference to the Acero `stddev()` function, as well as the values of the parameters passed to it.

### 7.2.4 Using Acero functions directly

We don't have to know anything at all about Acero functions in the typical case, where we know the R function we want to use, as arrow automatically translates it to the relevant Acero function if a binding does exist. But, what about if we want to use an Acero function which doesn't have an R equivalent to start from?

We can view the full list of Acero functions available to use in arrow by calling `list_compute_functions()`. At the time of writing there were 262 Acero functions available to use in R—the first 20 are shown below.

```
list_compute_functions() |>
  head(20)
```

```
 [1] "abs"                 "abs_checked"         "acos"
 [4] "acos_checked"        "add"                 "add_checked"
 [7] "all"                 "and"                 "and_kleene"
[10] "and_not"             "and_not_kleene"      "any"
[13] "approximate_median"  "array_filter"        "array_sort_indices"
[16] "array_take"          "ascii_capitalize"    "ascii_center"
[19] "ascii_is_alnum"      "ascii_is_alpha"
```

You can use these functions in your arrow dplyr pipelines by prefixing them with `"arrow_"`.

This isn't necessary when working with Acero functions which have a direct mapping to their R equivalents, which can be used instead. However, there are some niche use-cases where this could be helpful, such as if you want to use Acero options that don't exist in the R equivalent function, or if there is no equivalent R function at all.

Let's say that we wanted to do an analysis of the languages spoken by respondents in different areas. The columns we need for this analysis are:

- LANP - the language spoken in each area
- PWGTP - the weighting for that row in the dataset
- PUMA - a five-digit number representing the smallest geographical area represented in the data

Although the PUMA code is number, as it can begin with a zero, it's saved as a string. We know from having looked through the data that some rows in the dataset contain extra text, but for our analysis, we only want the rows in the dataset which contain only numbers in the PUMA column. We can use the Acero function utf8_is_digit(), which returns TRUE if a string contains only numbers and FALSE is there are any other characters in the string, to do this filtering.

```
open_dataset("data/person/") |>
  select(PUMA, LANP, PWGTP) |>
  filter(arrow_utf8_is_digit(PUMA))

FileSystemDataset (query)
PUMA: string
LANP: string
PWGTP: int32

* Filter: utf8_is_digit(PUMA)
See $.data for the source Arrow object
```

## 7.3   User-defined functions

Most functions you want to use exist both in R and in Acero, and the arrow package has bindings that map the R syntax to the Acero functions. The previous section showed how to use Acero functions that don't exist in R. But what if you want to use a R function which doesn't have an Acero equivalent?

In this case, you can create a **user-defined function** (UDF). User-defined functions allow arrow to use functions that don't have Acero bindings by calculating the results in your R session instead.

There is some additional processing overhead here because some of the calculation is being done by your R session and not by Acero, but it's a helpful tool to have in these circumstances.

### 7.3.1   An example of creating and using a UDF

You can create a UDF by using the function register_scalar_function(). Let's say we want to create a UDF which wraps the stringr function str_to_sentence(), which doesn't have an Acero equivalent. Here's an example of how it would look.

```
register_scalar_function(
  name = "str_to_sentence_udf",
  function(context, x) {
    stringr::str_to_sentence(x)
  },
  in_type = schema(
    x = string()
  ),
  out_type = string(),
  auto_convert = TRUE
)
```

Let's walk through that one part at a time. The first thing we need to do is define the name we'd like to use to call the function later—in this case, `str_to_sentence_udf`. Next, define the function itself. The first argument must always be `context`—this is used by the C++ code to store metadata to help it convert data between R and C++, but you don't need to do anything here manually other than name it as the first argument to your function. Next, define an argument which will be the columns in your dataset to use in the calculation, and any other values you need. In our case, we want the column representing the original string, which we've called x.

The body of the function itself is identical to when we defined it as an R function. The parameters `in_type` and `out_type` control the arrow data types of the input and output columns. Here, we provide a schema to `in_type` so that we can map function argument names to types, and we give a data type to `out_type`.

The `auto_convert` argument controls whether arrow automatically converts the inputs to R vectors or not. The default value, `FALSE`, means that inputs to your R function will be Arrow objects. In our example, this would mean that x would come in as an Arrow Array of type `string()`. But we want an R vector for x so that we can pass it to the stringr function. We could call `as.vector()` on x to convert the Array into an R vector, or we can do what we've done in this example and set `auto_convert = TRUE` to handle that for us. Setting `auto_convert = TRUE` also handles the return value conversion back to Arrow data for us.

Let's take a look at how this UDF works with our data.

```
pums_person |>
  select(SOCP) |>
  mutate(SOCP = str_to_sentence_udf(SOCP)) |>
  head() |>
  collect()
```

```
# A tibble: 6 x 1
  SOCP
  <chr>
1 Mgr-property, real estate, and community association managers
2 Edu-postsecondary teachers
3 <NA>
4 Unemployed, with no work experience in the last 5 years**
5 Eat-dishwashers
6 Med-registered nurses
```

## 7.3.2   Using UDFs for regression model predictions

Another example where UDFs can be useful is where you've created a model based on a
subset of your data and you want to use it to make predictions. Let's say we've created a
linear model, using education and employment status to predict hours worked per week for
respondents in 2018. When creating this model we aren't using the standard `stats::lm()`
because our data is weighted. The **survey** package has an equivalent regression function
`survey::svyglm()` which applies the weights in the weight column during the regression.
This isn't strictly necesary for the demonstration here, but it does show how UDFs work
not just with base R functions or functions in the tidyverse, but any R code that you come
up with.

```
model_data <- open_dataset("data/person/") |>
    filter(year == 2018) |>
    filter(AGEP >= 16, AGEP < 65, !is.na(COW)) |>
    transmute(
      self_employed = str_detect(as.character(COW), "Self-employed"),
      edu = case_when(
        grepl("bachelor|associate|professional|doctorate|master", SCHL,
        TRUE) ~
          "College or higher",
        grepl("college", SCHL, TRUE) ~
          "Some college",
        grepl("High school graduate|high school diploma|GED", SCHL, TRUE) ~
          "High school",
        TRUE ~ "Less than High school"
      ),
      hours_worked = WKHP,
      PWGTP = PWGTP
    ) |>
    collect()

hours_worked_model <- survey::svyglm(
  hours_worked ~ self_employed * edu,
  design = survey::svydesign(ids = ~1, weights = ~PWGTP, data = model_data)
)
summary(hours_worked_model)

Call:
svyglm(formula = hours_worked ~ self_employed * edu, design =
survey::svydesign(ids = ~1,
    weights = ~PWGTP, data = model_data))

Survey design:
survey::svydesign(ids = ~1, weights = ~PWGTP, data = model_data)

Coefficients:
                                           Estimate Std. Error t value
                                           Pr(>|t|)
(Intercept)                                40.87539    0.01705 2397.62
<2e-16
```

```
self_employedTRUE                              -1.63441    0.08327  -19.63
<2e-16
eduHigh school                                 -2.35634    0.03073  -76.67
<2e-16
eduLess than High school                       -6.66604    0.05241 -127.19
<2e-16
eduSome college                                -3.52614    0.03320 -106.22
<2e-16
self_employedTRUE:eduHigh school                2.61369    0.14297   18.28
<2e-16
self_employedTRUE:eduLess than High school  3.72725    0.19556   19.06
<2e-16
self_employedTRUE:eduSome college               2.77875    0.15217   18.26
<2e-16

(Intercept)                                ***
self_employedTRUE                          ***
eduHigh school                             ***
eduLess than High school                   ***
eduSome college                            ***
self_employedTRUE:eduHigh school           ***
self_employedTRUE:eduLess than High school ***
self_employedTRUE:eduSome college          ***
---
Signif. codes:  0 '***' 0.001 '**' 0.01 '*' 0.05 '.' 0.1 ' ' 1

(Dispersion parameter for gaussian family taken to be 152.4535)

Number of Fisher Scoring iterations: 2
```

We can use this model to predict what our model would have predicted on this data if it were new data coming in. This is a little artificial since this is the same data that we used to build the model, though it's a good check to confirm that the modeling process doesn't have anything terribly off about it. Also, because we are predicting on the same data we fit this linear model on, this is going to be very close to the actual weighted means. We use the `predict` function to make these predictions and we also calculate the weighted mean for each group.

```
model_data$predicted <- predict(hours_worked_model, newdata = model_data)

model_data_summary <- model_data |>
  group_by(edu, self_employed) |>
  summarise(
    work_hours_mean = weighted.mean(hours_worked, w = PWGTP, na.rm = TRUE),
    work_hours_predicted = weighted.mean(predicted, w = PWGTP),
  )
```

And we can plot our model as well as the predictions to visualize what is going on. Here the underlying data is represented in the density curve—the taller the curve the more observations are at that point on the x-axis (hours worked per week). At the bottom the line represents the weighted mean and the diamond is the prediction from our model. And like we said above, we can confirm that the weighted means and the model predictions are incredibly close[5].

Let's say we want to use this model to predict working hours in Alaska in 2021. We can create a UDF which calls `predict()` to add the predicted commute time value to the data.

```
register_scalar_function(
  "predict_work_hours",
  function(context, edu, self_employed) {
    as.numeric(predict(
      hours_worked_model,
      newdata = data.frame(edu, self_employed)
    ))
  },
  in_type = schema(edu = string(), self_employed = boolean()),
  out_type = float64(),
  auto_convert = TRUE
)


modelled_data <- open_dataset("data/person/") |>
  filter(year == 2021, location == "ak") |>
  filter(AGEP >= 16, AGEP < 65, !is.na(COW)) |>
    transmute(
      self_employed = str_detect(as.character(COW), "Self-employed"),
      edu = case_when(
        grepl("bachelor|associate|professional|doctorate|master", SCHL,
        TRUE) ~
          "College or higher",
        grepl("college", SCHL, TRUE) ~
          "Some college",
        grepl("High school graduate|high school diploma|GED", SCHL, TRUE) ~
          "High school",
        TRUE ~ "Less than High school"
      ),
      hours_worked = WKHP,
      PWGTP = PWGTP,
      predicted = predict_work_hours(edu, self_employed),
    ) |>
  collect()
```

We are slightly off in most categories, but especially far off for high school and some college educated workers where we predict much lower working hours. Not totally surprising given our original model was built with all of the US and states differ considerably on this dimension.

Let's test that theory out: we can also re-use this UDF for any subset, including predicting on all of the US in 2021.

```
modelled_data <- open_dataset("data/person/") |>
  filter(year == 2021) |>
  filter(AGEP >= 16, AGEP < 65, !is.na(COW)) |>
```

---

[5]They better be very close since this is the same data the linear regression was fit with!

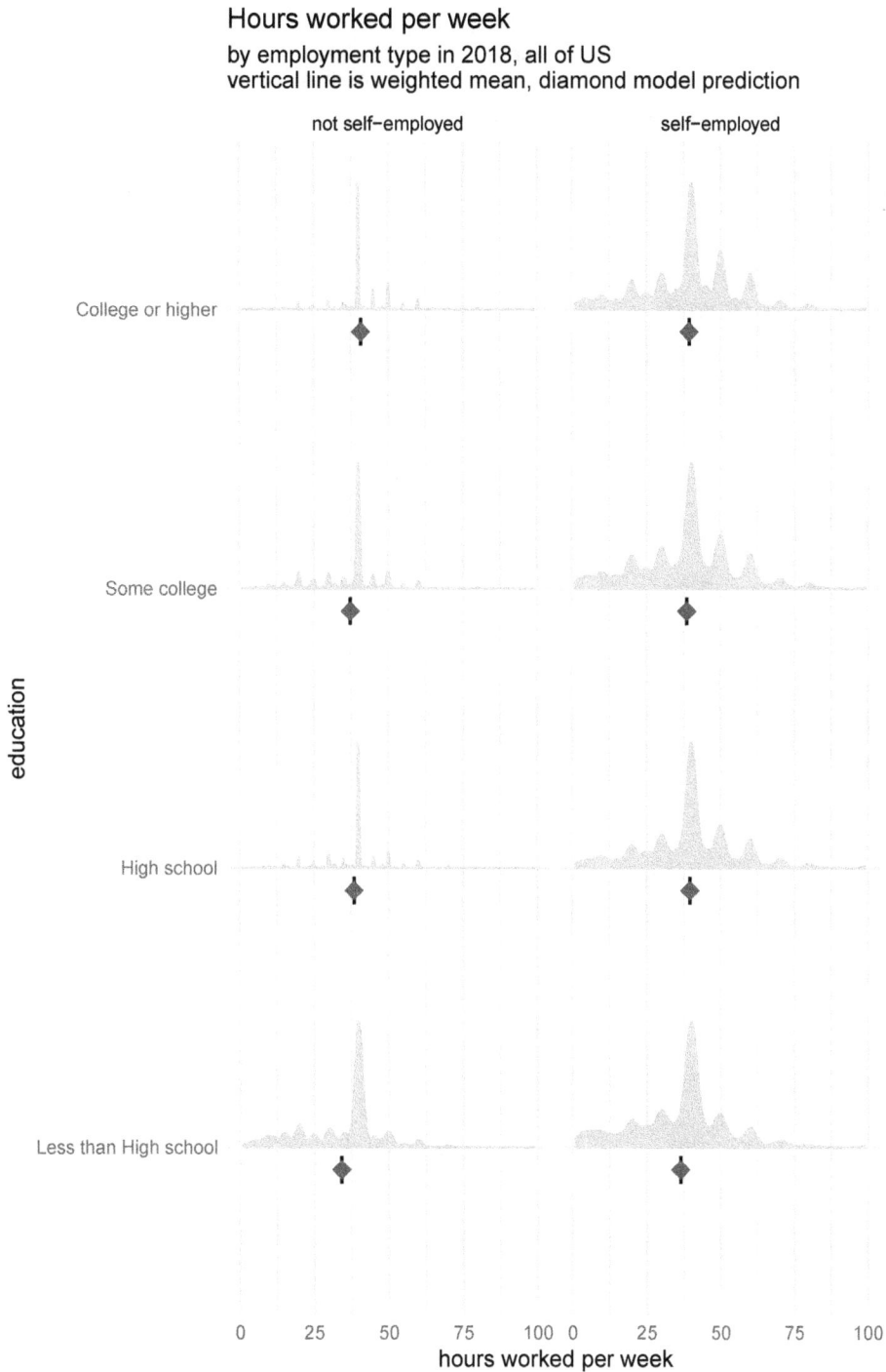

Figure 7.1: Hours worked per week by employment type in 2018 for all of the United States. The density curve is the raw data, the line at the bottom the weighted mean and the diamond at the bottom is the weighted mean of the model predictions.

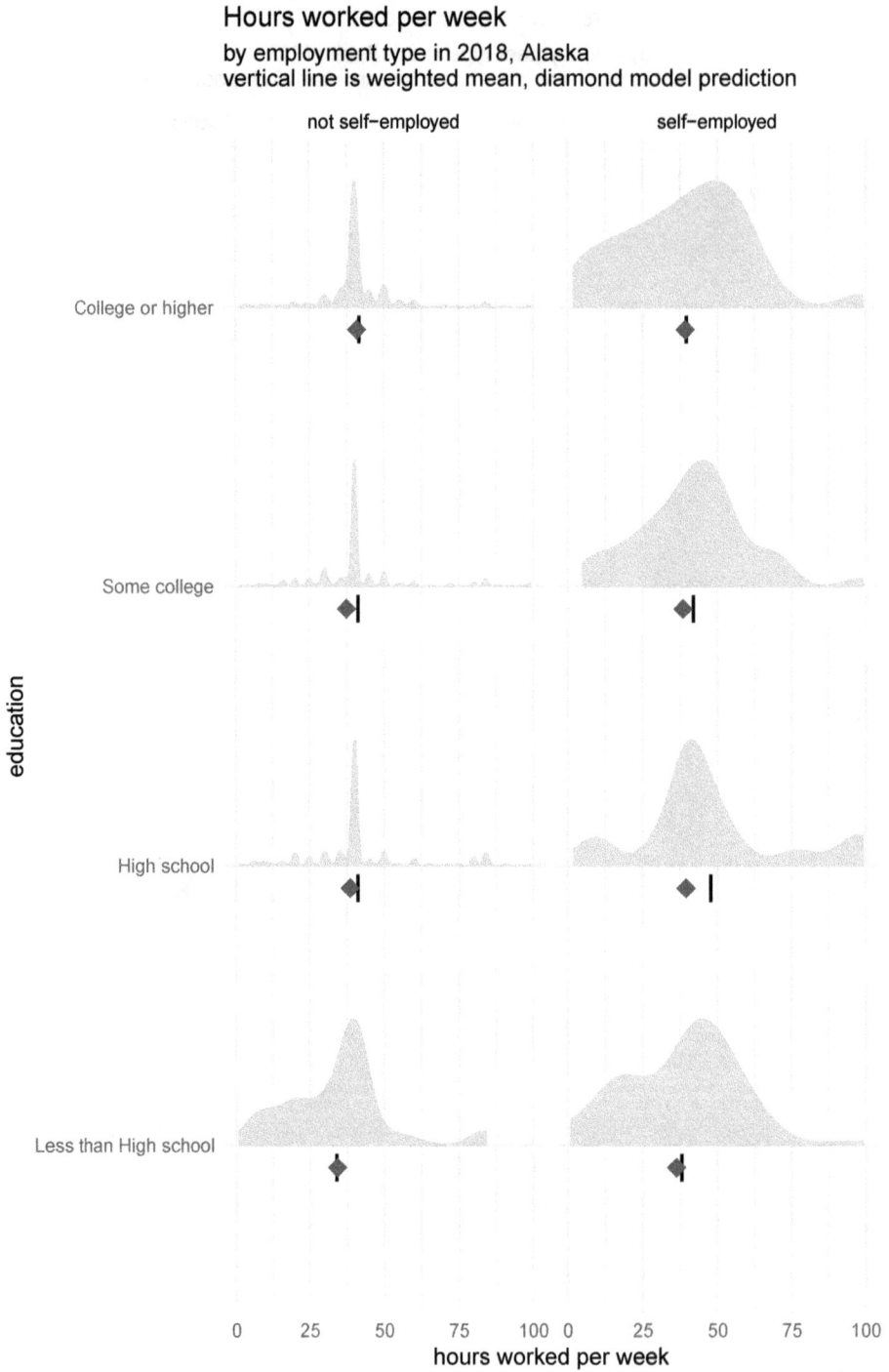

Figure 7.2: Hours worked per week by employment type in 2021 for Alaska. The density curve is the raw data, the line at the bottom the weighted mean and the diamond at the bottom is the weighted mean of the model predictions.

```
  transmute(
    self_employed = str_detect(as.character(COW), "Self-employed"),
    edu = case_when(
      grepl("bachelor|associate|professional|doctorate|master", SCHL,
      TRUE) ~
        "College or higher",
      grepl("college", SCHL, TRUE) ~
        "Some college",
      grepl("High school graduate|high school diploma|GED", SCHL, TRUE) ~
        "High school",
      TRUE ~ "Less than High school"
    ),
    hours_worked = WKHP,
    PWGTP = PWGTP,
    predicted = predict_work_hours(edu, self_employed),
  ) |>
collect()


modelled_data |> head()

# A tibble: 6 x 5
  self_employed edu                   hours_worked PWGTP predicted
  <lgl>         <chr>                        <int> <int>     <dbl>
1 FALSE         Some college                    40    38      37.3
2 FALSE         High school                     40   151      38.5
3 FALSE         Some college                    40    16      37.3
4 FALSE         Less than High school           80    75      34.2
5 FALSE         Less than High school           NA    60      34.2
6 FALSE         Less than High school           50    15      34.2
```

And how good were our predictions?

And we can see the fit is slightly better, though we still slightly over predict, particularly for self-employed workers. From here we might explore fitting a multi-level model with varying slopes or intercepts for each state or add more predictors to our model. But no matter what we choose, we can use UDFs to do prediction like we did here.

## 7.3.3 How do UDFs work under the hood?

UDFs only work on scalar functions—functions which take one row of data as input and return one row of data as output. Acero does not currently support user-defined aggregation functions. For example, you could create a UDF which calculates the square of a number, but you can't create one which calculates the median value in a column of data. These functions also cannot depend on other values, so you can't write a UDF which implements **lag()** or **lead()** which calculate a value based on the previous or next row in the data.

Because the UDF code is run in your R session, you won't be able to take advantage of some of the features of arrow, such as being able to run code on multiple CPU cores, or the faster speed of executing C++ code. You'll also be slowed down a little by the fact that arrow has to convert back and forth between R and arrow, and R is single-threaded, so each calculation is run on one chunk of data at a time instead of parallelized across many chunks at once.

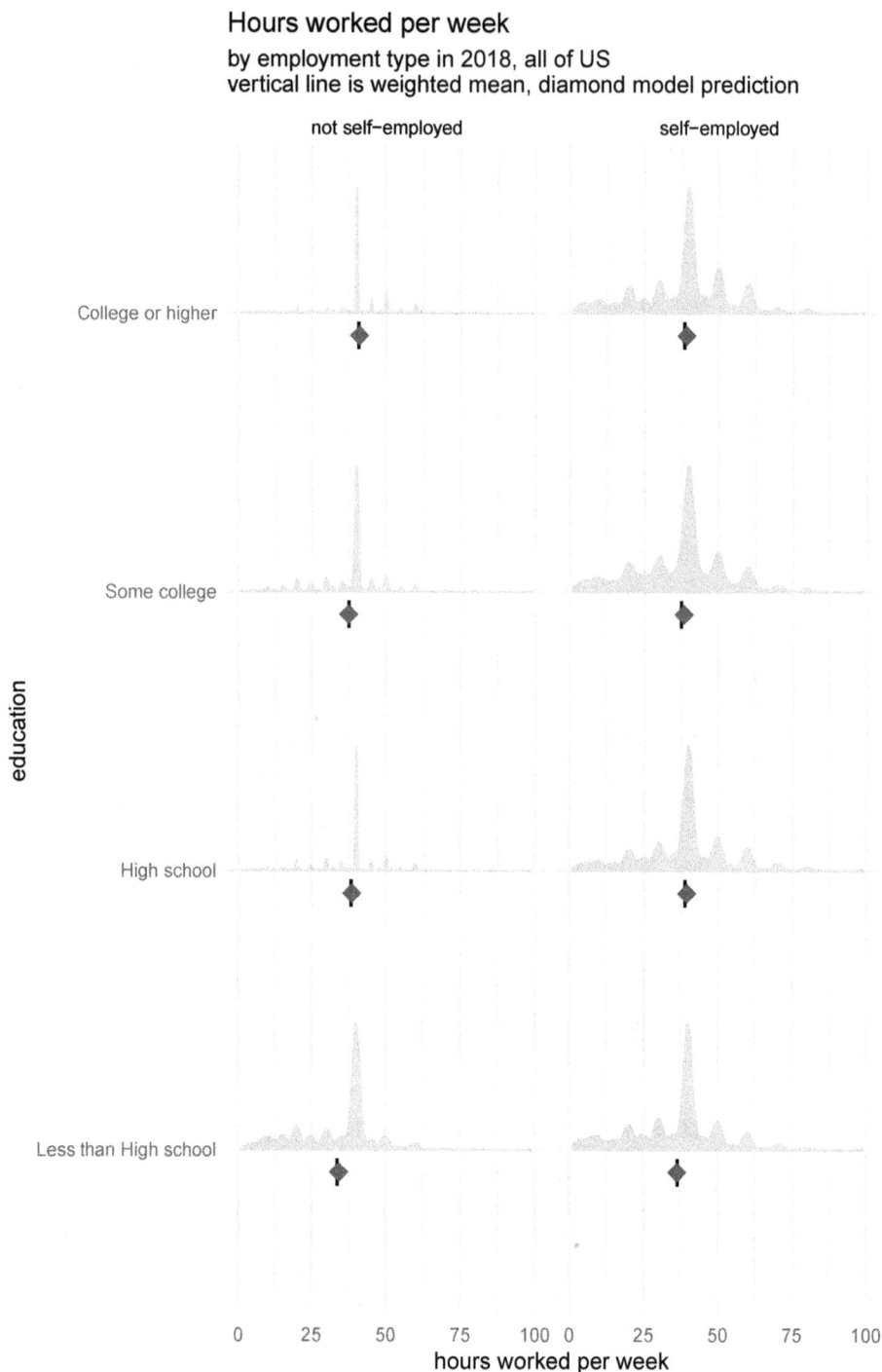

Figure 7.3: Hours worked per week by employment type in 2021 for all of the United States. The density curve is the raw data, the line at the bottom the weighted mean and the diamond at the bottom is the weighted mean of the model predictions.

The workflow for writing and using UDFs can feel a bit clunky, as it's pretty different to how we typically work with data in R; for example, we don't normally have to specify input and output types, or just work on 1 row of data at a time.

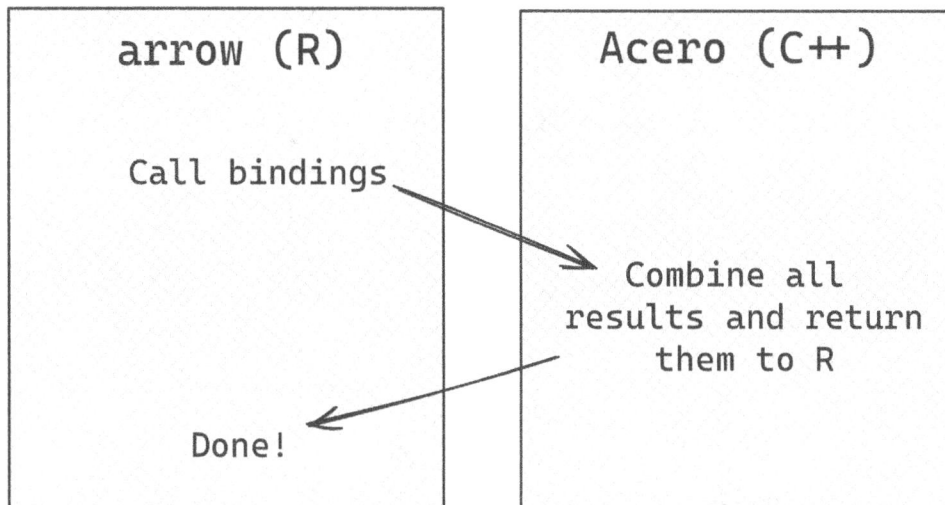

Figure 7.4: How Acero bindings work

The extra steps needed are because we are working more directly with Acero, the part of the Arrow C++ library that runs the data manipulation queries, and as Acero is written in C++ we have to make sure we are giving it the correct information to work with.

C++ is strongly typed, which means that when a variable is created, you also have to declare its type, which cannot be changed later. This is quite different to R, where, for example, you can create an integer variable which later becomes a double. In Acero, the fact that C++ variables require a type declaration means that Acero functions can only run on data where the data types in the columns perfectly match the data types specified for the function parameters when the function is being defined. What this means is that when we write a UDF, we need to specify the input and output types, so that the code under the hood can properly create the correct C++ function that can run on those data types.

Another thing that might seem unusual is that UDFs are limited to processing one row at a time. It's pretty common in R to work with vectorized functions—those that can operate on multiple rows at the same time—and there are lots of places in Arrow where things are designed to be able to be run in parallel. So why not here? The answer is memory management. When Acero is processing queries, it avoids reading all of the data into memory unless it's absolutely necessary; for example, sorting data in row order requires Acero to pull the full column into memory to be able to determine the ordering. Usually though, if you're reading a dataset, doing some processing, and then writing it back to disk, this is done one piece at a time; Acero monitors the available memory and how much memory is being used and then reads and writes to disk in chunks that won't exceed these limits. This concept is called "backpressure", a term which originally was used to describe controlling the flow of liquid through pipes! In this context, backpressure means that if the queue of data that is waiting to be written after processing is at risk of growing too large for the available memory, Acero will slow down how much data is being read in, to prevent using too much memory and crashing. For compatibility with this piece-wise reading and writing,

UDFs need to be able to operate in smaller chunks of data, which is why they can only use scalar functions and run on one row of data at a time.

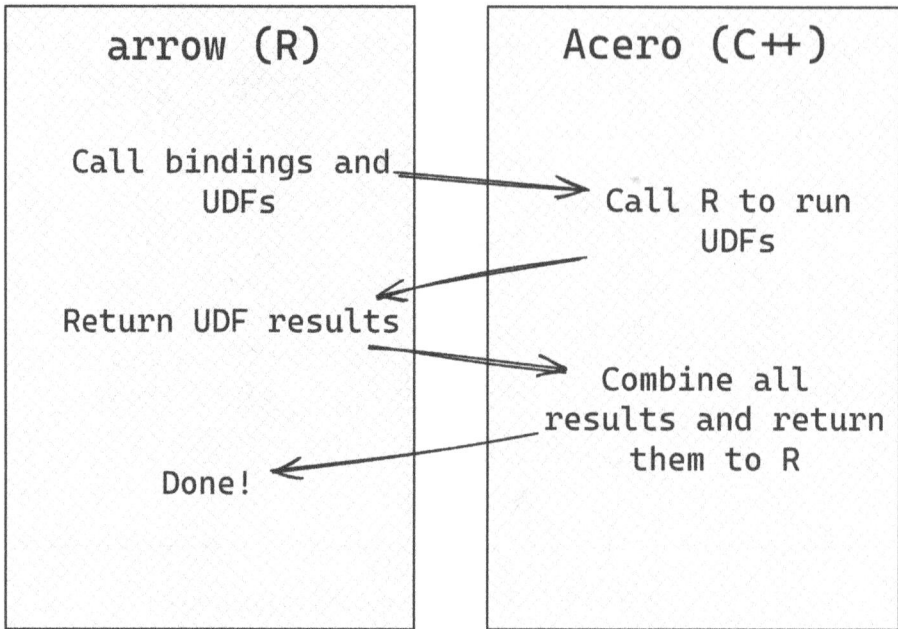

Figure 7.5: How UDFs work

Most of the time you don't need to worry about these internal details of Acero! However, when working with UDFs, we're working a lot closer to Acero's internals, and need to step into these deeper waters.

## 7.4  DuckDB

Although arrow implements a lot of the dplyr API, you may want to work with functions from other packages which haven't been implemented in arrow or can't be written as UDFs. For example, if you want to change the shape of your data, you might want to use `tidyr::pivot_longer()`, but this is not yet supported in arrow.

```
library(tidyr)

pums_person |>
  group_by(location) |>
  summarize(
    max_commute = max(JWMNP, na.rm = TRUE),
    min_commute = min(JWMNP, na.rm = TRUE)
  ) |>
  pivot_longer(!location, names_to = "metric")
```

```
Error in UseMethod("pivot_longer"): no applicable method for 'pivot_longer'
applied to an object of class "arrow_dplyr_query"
```

Don't worry though! We mentioned that arrow is designed with interoperability in mind, and we can take advantage of that here. The **duckdb** package allows working with large datasets, and importantly in this case, has an implementation of `pivot_longer()`.

In our example here, we can pass the data to duckdb, pivot it, and return it to arrow to continue with our analysis.

```
pums_person |>
  group_by(location) |>
  summarize(
    max_commute = max(JWMNP, na.rm = TRUE),
    min_commute = min(JWMNP, na.rm = TRUE)
  ) |>
  to_duckdb() |> # send data to duckdb
  pivot_longer(!location, names_to = "metric") |>
  to_arrow() |> # return data back to arrow
  collect()
```

```
# A tibble: 104 x 3
   location metric       value
   <chr>    <chr>        <int>
 1 al       max_commute    194
 2 ca       max_commute    178
 3 fl       max_commute    193
 4 il       max_commute    197
 5 me       max_commute    199
 6 md       max_commute    182
 7 ne       max_commute    163
 8 ny       max_commute    195
 9 oh       max_commute    183
10 ct       max_commute    179
# i 94 more rows
```

We start off with an Arrow Dataset, which is turned into a dataset query when we call `summarize()`. We're still using lazy evaluation here, and no calculations have been run on our data.

When we call `to_duckdb()`, this function creates a virtual DuckDB table whose data points to the Arrow object. We then call `pivot_longer()`, which runs in duckdb.

Only when `collect()` is called at the end does the data pipeline run. Because we are passing a pointer to where the data is stored in memory, the data has been passed rapidly between Arrow and DuckDB without the need for serialization and deserialization resulting in copying things back and forth, and slowing things down. We'll look under the hood in Chapter 8 to show how Arrow enables this form of efficient communication between different projects.

The arrow and duckdb R packages have a lot of overlapping functionality, and both have features and functions the other doesn't. We choose to focus on the complementarities of the two packages, both for practical and personal reasons. Since Arrow is focused on improving interoperability, we tend to take a "yes, and..." approach to solutions. We also have enjoyed collaborating with the DuckDB maintainers over the years and appreciate the work they do.

In any case, it would be hard to make a clear, simple statement like "use arrow for X and duckdb for Y," if for no other reason than that both projects are in active development, and any claim would quickly become outdated. For example, arrow has historically had better dplyr support than duckdb because duckdb relied on dbplyr to translate dplyr verbs into SQL, while the arrow developers invested heavily in mapping R functions to Acero functions for a higher fidelity translation. On the other hand, Acero does not currently have a SQL interface. But there are no technical limitations preventing duckdb from improving dplyr support—and by the time you are reading this, they very well may have![6]—nor from there being a SQL interface to arrow.

For most applications, you could use either arrow or duckdb just fine. But, if you do encounter cases where one package supports something the other doesn't, the smooth integration between arrow and duckdb means can leverage the best of both. For example, suppose you want to use SQL to query a bucket of Parquet files in Google Cloud Storage, as in our example in Chapter 6. At the time of writing, the arrow R package doesn't support SQL, and DuckDB doesn't support GCS. You could use arrow to connect to GCS and read the Parquet files, and then duckdb to run the SQL.

To run SQL, we need to specify a `table_name` in `to_duckdb()` so that we can reference it in our SQL statement. Then we use `dbplyr::remote_con()` to pull out the duckdb connection, followed by `DBI::dbGetQuery()` to send the query and return the result. Something like this:

```
open_dataset("gs://anonymous@scaling-arrow-pums/person/") |>
  to_duckdb(table_name = "pums8") |>
  dbplyr::remote_con() |>
  DBI::dbGetQuery("
    SELECT
      year,
      SUM(AGEP * PWGTP) / SUM(PWGTP) AS mean_age
    FROM (SELECT * FROM pums8 WHERE location = 'wa')
    GROUP BY year")
```

To reiterate: for most workloads of the nature we've been focusing on in this book—analytic queries on larger-than-memory datasets—either package would be a great choice. We like both, and we are excited to watch them become even better going forward. Your choice is a matter of preference more than anything. You may observe subtle differences in the user interface (the functions and arguments), or the documentation, or user and developer communities, that may lead you to prefer one or the other. And as we have shown, you can easily complement one with the other when you need, so it isn't a choice that locks you into one world or another.

## 7.5  Extending arrow and geospatial data

At this point, we've seen that the Arrow specification covers a wide range of data types which are commonly encountered in data storage systems, to maximize interoperability. That said, there are always going to be more data types out there for specialist uses.

---

[6]Indeed, see duckplyr: https://duckdblabs.github.io/duckplyr/.

### 7.5.1 Extension types

One example of specialist data types is geospatial data.

Accurate representations of metadata are important with geospatial data. There are different coordinate reference systems (CRS) which can be used to represent geospatial data, and knowing which one has been used is crucial when combining data from multiple sources.

WGS 84 (EPSG:4326)

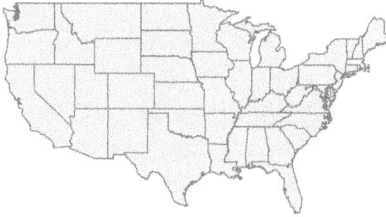

NAD83 / Conus Albers (EPSG:5070)

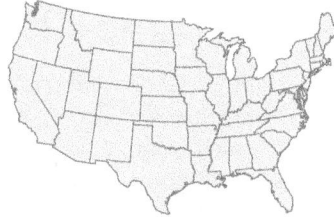

US National Atlas Equal Area (EPSG:2163)  UTM Zone 11N (ESPG:2955)

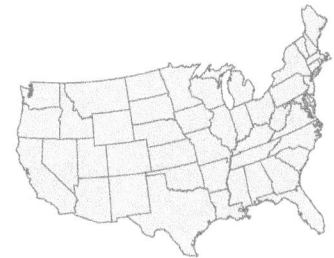

Figure 7.6: Plots of four different Coordinate Reference Systems for the continental United States

Saving geospatial data to Arrow format isn't as simple as taking the data and mapping values to the equivalent Arrow data types. Many geospatial applications have custom data types used to describe the location and shape being represented in the data. These are known as geometries, and can be defined using points, lines, polygons, and other things. These geometries are often stored along with their associated attributes, descriptive information relating to them.

Although these non-standard data types don't have direct Arrow equivalents, they can be implemented using extension types. Extension types allow you to create custom predefined data types. For example, you could have a `location` data type for which each value consists of a `latitude` and `longitude` float value. That said, there's a huge range of possibilities for representing geospatial data, and using standardized formats can speed things up when sharing data between platforms.

### 7.5.2 Arrow format with existing storage formats

There are a multitude of different systems for working with geospatial data. Many of the challenges of geospatial data mirror the challenges found working with larger datasets in general: the need for efficient interchange between systems, performance issues on large, complex, or multi-file datasets, and different implementations of overlapping ideas.

### 7.5.3   GeoParquet

GeoParquet was designed to address these issues. GeoParquet provides a standard format for storing geospatial data on disk and can be used with arrow to then represent geospatial data in-memory. The GeoParquet format allows geospatial data to be stored in Parquet files. While it was already possible to store data in Parquet files and have lossless roundtripping between R and Parquet, GeoParquet has the added advantage of being a standardized format for this in the form of a file-level metadata specification.

Working with data in GeoParquet format allows people to take advantage of the same benefits that come with working with any data in Parquet format; the row and column chunk metadata which is an inherent part of Parquet means that filtering on this data can be done without needing to read all data into memory. Parquet's encoding and compression means that GeoParquet files tend to take up less space on disk than similar formats.

Arrow can read GeoParquet files and preserve the metadata necessary to work with geospatial data efficiently. At the time of writing, there is also a nascent project called GeoArrow designed to make interoperation even easier and more efficient. GeoArrow aims to use the formats and approach of GeoParquet, so it should be very similar.

#### 7.5.3.1   GeoParquet data

The GeoParquet specification has two components: the format of the metadata and then the format of the data itself. There are two levels of metadata:

1. file-level metadata which contains information about the version of the GeoParquet specification that the saved data conforms to and which column is the primary geometry column
2. column-level metadata about the individual geometry columns

To make this concrete, we will use geospatial definitions for PUMAs (we will discuss what these are in more detail in Section 7.5.5). This Parquet file has a number of standard columns along with one column, `geometry`, that includes the geospatial specifications: in this case, polygons and multi polygons, which are the shapes of the PUMAs.

```
# Read in the puma geoparquet, mark it as such with SF
PUMA <- read_parquet(
  "data/PUMA2013_2022.parquet",
  as_data_frame = FALSE
)
```

#### 7.5.3.2   Column-level metadata

The column-level GeoParquet metadata stores two different types of information:

1. What kind of geometry is represented in the column, e.g. point, polygon, linestring, etc
2. Further metadata about that column, for example, the CRS.

### 7.5.3.3 Data format

GeoParquet specifies two different ways of representing geometry data: serialized encoding and native encodings. Native encodings are where this data is stored in Arrow data structures. Serialized encodings are where data is stored in existing geospatial formats. Well-known binary (WKB) data is converted into Arrow Binary and LargeBinary data and Well-known Text (WKT) as Arrow Utf8 or LargeUtf8. This is part of the GeoParquet specification to ensure that this metadata can be preserved without needing to fully convert to the native encoding; however, it can be slower to work with.

Native encoding allows people to full take advantage of working with Arrow data types and capabilities. It provides concrete Arrow data structure to store geometry data in. For example, co-ordinates are stored in one of two Arrow structures. The "separated" approach saves coordinate values in separate Arrow Arrays; one for x values, and one for y values. The "interleaved" approach saves co-ordinate values in a FixedSizeList, and allows x and y values to be stored in an alternating pattern. Other types of geometries are stored in Arrow Arrays or nested ListArrays with a given structure.

For our example, most of the columns are standard types we've seen already. But the `geometry` column is the type `binary` and specifically the WKB type. Though this looks complicated, it's very similar to other types: the column is an array of values, effectively a vector in R. The difference is that instead of containing data that are one string per row (that is: UTF8 encoded bytes), this data is one chunk of binary data per row. This binary data is WKB data, which packages like `sf` can understand.

```
schema(PUMA)
```

```
Schema
location: string
STATEFIP: string
YEAR: int32
PUMA: string
GEOID: string
NAMELSAD: string
MTFCC: string
FUNCSTAT: string
ALAND: double
AWATER: double
INTPTLAT: string
INTPTLON: string
geometry: binary


See $metadata for additional Schema metadata
```

There is also metadata about this column. The most important thing that we care about here is the CRS.

```
schema(PUMA)$metadata$geo
```

[1] "{\"primary_column\": \"geometry\", \"columns\": {\"geometry\":
{\"encoding\": \"WKB\", \"crs\": {\"$schema\":
\"https://proj.org/schemas/v0.7/projjson.schema.json\", \"type\":
\"GeographicCRS\", \"name\": \"NAD83\", \"datum\": {\"type\":
\"GeodeticReferenceFrame\", \"name\": \"North American Datum 1983\",
\"ellipsoid\": {\"name\": \"GRS 1980\", \"semi_major_axis\": 6378137,
\"inverse_flattening\": 298.257222101}}, \"coordinate_system\":
{\"subtype\": \"ellipsoidal\", \"axis\": [{\"name\": \"Geodetic latitude\",
\"abbreviation\": \"Lat\", \"direction\": \"north\", \"unit\": \"degree\"},
{\"name\": \"Geodetic longitude\", \"abbreviation\": \"Lon\",
\"direction\": \"east\", \"unit\": \"degree\"}]}, \"scope\": \"Geodesy.\",
\"area\": \"North America - onshore and offshore: Canada - Alberta; British
Columbia; Manitoba; New Brunswick; Newfoundland and Labrador; Northwest
Territories; Nova Scotia; Nunavut; Ontario; Prince Edward Island; Quebec;
Saskatchewan; Yukon. Puerto Rico. United States (USA) - Alabama; Alaska;
Arizona; Arkansas; California; Colorado; Connecticut; Delaware; Florida;
Georgia; Hawaii; Idaho; Illinois; Indiana; Iowa; Kansas; Kentucky;
Louisiana; Maine; Maryland; Massachusetts; Michigan; Minnesota;
Mississippi; Missouri; Montana; Nebraska; Nevada; New Hampshire; New
Jersey; New Mexico; New York; North Carolina; North Dakota; Ohio; Oklahoma;
Oregon; Pennsylvania; Rhode Island; South Carolina; South Dakota;
Tennessee; Texas; Utah; Vermont; Virginia; Washington; West Virginia;
Wisconsin; Wyoming. US Virgin Islands. British Virgin Islands.\", \"bbox\":
{\"south_latitude\": 14.92, \"west_longitude\": 167.65, \"north_latitude\":
86.45, \"east_longitude\": -40.73}, \"id\": {\"authority\": \"EPSG\",
\"code\": 4269}}, \"geometry_types\": [\"MultiPolygon\", \"Polygon\"],
\"bbox\": [-179.231086, 13.234188999999999, 179.859681, 71.439786]}},
\"version\": \"1.0.0\", \"creator\": {\"library\": \"geopandas\",
\"version\": \"0.14.3\"}}"

This is a `projjson` encoding of the CRS for the `geometry` column. This encoding is text, which is actually JSON.

```
jsonlite::fromJSON(schema(PUMA)$metadata$geo)
```

```
$primary_column
[1] "geometry"


$columns
$columns$geometry
$columns$geometry$encoding
[1] "WKB"


$columns$geometry$crs
$columns$geometry$crs$`$schema`
[1] "https://proj.org/schemas/v0.7/projjson.schema.json"


$columns$geometry$crs$type
[1] "GeographicCRS"


$columns$geometry$crs$name
[1] "NAD83"
```

```
$columns$geometry$crs$datum
$columns$geometry$crs$datum$type
...
```

And from this we can see that the CRS for our PUMAs is NAD83. We will use this later when we plot the data.

### 7.5.4 Connecting the pieces

We've already read in our geospatial data, and have our PUMS dataset to analyze and plot, and now we need to follow a few more steps to make sure that R plotting libraries like ggplot2 can work with this data.

When this book was being written, there were already nascent projects to make this smoother. sfarrow[7] has tools for reading and writing geospatial data using arrow and the r package geoarrow[8] is under development to make it easier to load data that conforms to GeoParquet and GeoArrow standards.

Today, however, we need to do a couple more things before we can work with it further and use sf and ggplot2 to plot this: make sure that our CRS is set correctly and pulling the data into R. To do both of these, we create a helper function. This helper function ensures that we use the CRS we saw the data had above. It also sets the bounding box and center so that the entirety of the United States is laid out correctly.[9] Finally, we pull the data into R and set the correct geometry column to use.

```
correct_projection <- function(PUMA, crs = "NAD83") {
  PUMA_df <- collect(PUMA)
  # set the geometry column, but we also need to manually
  # extract the CRS from the geoparquet metadata
  PUMA_df <- sf::st_sf(PUMA_df, sf_column_name = "geometry",
                       crs = crs)

  # Move the bounding box + center of the projection so that
  # Alaska is plotted together
  proj <- paste(
    "+proj=aea",
    "+lat_1=29.5",
    "+lat_2=45.5",
    "+lat_0=23",
    "+lon_0=-96",
    "+x_0=0",
    "+y_0=0",
    "+ellps=GRS80",
    "+towgs84=0,0,0,0,0,0,0",
    "+units=m +no_defs"
  )
  PUMA_df$geometry <- st_transform(PUMA_df$geometry, crs = proj)

  PUMA_df
}
```

---

[7]https://github.com/wcjochem/sfarrow

[8]https://github.com/geoarrow/geoarrow-r

[9]Without this, some of the Aleutian Islands which are to the west of the 180th meridian will be plotted to the east of the rest of the United States.

### 7.5.5   Enhancing PUMS data with GeoParquet PUMAs data

Putting this all together, let's try making a plot[10] showing different languages spoken throughout the United States. The analysis we will build up is the percentage of speakers for languages spoken in the US. We will then plot this data, subsetting to a few interesting languages depending on what region we are plotting. In the PUMS dataset, the smallest geographic area is called a PUMA (Public Use Microdata Areas)[11].[12] These PUMAs are designed to have approximately 100,000 people in them, and must be within a single state.

As always, we start with our PUMS dataset. We build up a `dplyr` query to clean some data inconsistencies, such as varying capitalization, then group by language and PUMA by state and year, and calculate how many speakers of each language there are in each PUMA. We can see that this returns a data frame with one row per PUMA and language, with the number of speakers and the proportion of speakers whose primary language is not English compared to the overall population.

```
pums_person <- open_dataset("./data/person")

puma_by_langauge <- pums_person |>
  filter(year == 2018) |>
  mutate(
    language = tolower(LANP),
    language = case_when(
      is.na(language) ~ "english",
      TRUE ~ language
    )
  ) |>
  filter(language != "english") |>
  group_by(location, PUMA, year, language) |>
  summarize(
    n_people = sum(PWGTP)
  ) |>
  group_by(location, PUMA, year) |>
  mutate(
    prop_speaker = n_people / sum(n_people),
  ) |>
  ungroup()

puma_by_langauge |>
  head() |>
  collect()
```

```
# A tibble: 6 x 6
  location PUMA   year language    n_people prop_speaker
  <chr>    <chr> <int> <chr>          <int>        <dbl>
1 ca       03718  2018 spanish        35606        0.601
2 ca       07502  2018 chinese         9490        0.251
```

---

[10] This type of plot is called a choropleth where a geographic representation is colored or shaded to show different values in different areas.

[11] https://www.census.gov/programs-surveys/geography/guidance/geo-areas/pumas.html

[12] There is also a more detailed description of PUMAs in Kyle Walker's *Analyzing US Census Data: Methods, Maps, and Models in R*: https://walker-data.com/census-r/introduction-to-census-microdata.html#what-is-a-puma

| 3 | ca | 07305 | 2018 | german | 810 | 0.0206 |
| 4 | ca | 01100 | 2018 | spanish | 30125 | 0.902 |
| 5 | ca | 08504 | 2018 | vietnamese | 20011 | 0.217 |
| 6 | ca | 06509 | 2018 | spanish | 71701 | 0.913 |

And then we can take that data, join it to our arrow table of PUMAs and plot it using ggplot2. There is one other cleaning step we need, though, and we've factored it out into a `fill_pumas()` function. The function is a wrapper around some dplyr joins to make it so that each PUMA has one row for each language. Because many languages are not spoken at all in many PUMAs, we need to do this so that the plots still show those PUMAs as 0, not NA.

```
fill_pumas <- function(query) {
  # unique combination of every state + puma + year
  unique_pumas <- query |>
    distinct(location, PUMA, year) |>
    # add `key` as a constant so we can join with `unique_languages`
    mutate(key = 1)

  # all of the languages
  unique_languages <- query |>
    distinct(language) |>
    mutate(key = 1)

  # crossed together
  pumas_languages <- unique_pumas |>
    full_join(unique_languages) |>
    select(-key)

  # return the original query with all of the
  # unique combinations, when those values are
  # NA, make them 0
  query |>
    right_join(pumas_languages) |>
    mutate(
      n_people = coalesce(n_people, 0),
      prop_speaker = coalesce(prop_speaker, 0)
    )
}
```

Note that, as we discussed in Section 3.5, none of the steps in `fill_pumas()` calls `collect()` or `compute()`: they are all adding steps to the query without evaluating it.

*Now* we're ready to plot.

```
puma_by_langauge |>
  filter(language %in% c("german", "spanish", "french", "navajo")) |>
  fill_pumas() |>
  inner_join(
    PUMA,
    by = c("year" = "YEAR", "location" = "location", "PUMA" = "PUMA")
  ) |>
  correct_projection() |>
```

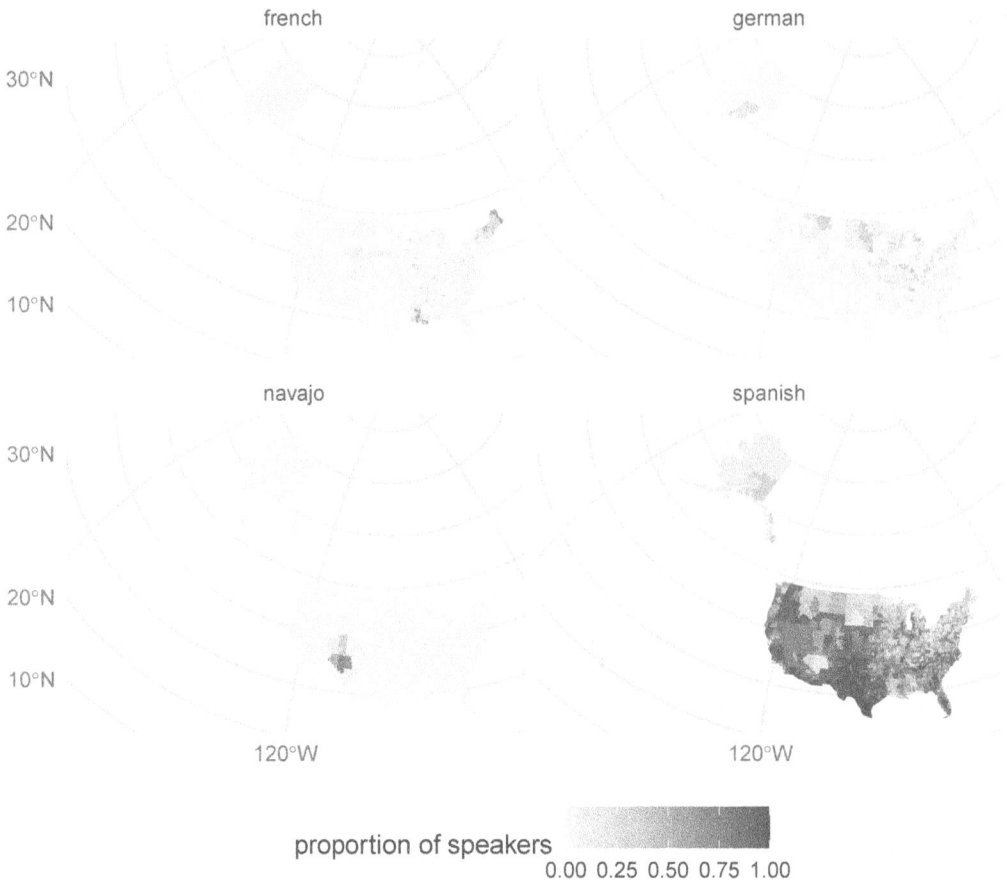

Figure 7.7: Proportion of speakers whose primary language is not English by language across the US by PUMA for German, French, Navajo, and Spanish

```
ggplot() +
geom_sf(aes(geometry = geometry, fill = prop_speaker),
        lwd = 0) +
coord_sf(crs = "+proj=laea +lon_0=-98 +lat_0=39.5") +
facet_wrap(vars(language), ncol = 2) +
scale_fill_distiller(type = "seq", direction = 1,
                     palette = "Greys",
                     name = "proportion of speakers") +
theme_minimal() +
theme(legend.position = "bottom") +
labs(
  title = "Proportion of non-English speakers by language",
  subtitle = "across the US by PUMA"
)
```

We can clearly see some patterns of migration: French is spoken in parts of northern Maine and Louisiana; German is spoken in the Midwest, especially in the upper Midwest and intermountain west.

---

💡 **Tip**

That plotting code might look intimidating at first, but most of it is to add theming and to get the projection on the globe. Breaking this down chunk by chunk:

```
ggplot() +
```

The standard start to `ggplot2`.

```
  geom_sf(
    aes(geometry = geometry, fill = prop_speaker),
    lwd = 0
  ) +
```

Set the `geom` to be a map, with the color proportion of speaker. Also set the line width of the outlines of each PUMA to be none.

```
  coord_sf(crs = "+proj=laea +lon_0=-98 +lat_0=39.5") +
```

This shifts the projection slightly to be as if it were on a globe.

```
  facet_wrap(vars(language), ncol = 2) +
```

Making small multiples for each language

```
  scale_fill_distiller(type = "seq", direction = 1,
    palette = "Greys", name = "proportion of speakers") +
  theme_minimal() +
  theme(legend.position = "bottom") +
  labs(
    title = "Proportion of non-English speakers by language",
    subtitle = "across the US by PUMA"
  )
```

And finally, the theme, labels, title, and color scale.

---

With geospatial plotting, the more detailed a plot is, the larger amount of data needs to be processed to make the plot. At that scale, it can be hard to see just how detailed this map ends up being. Not only are the coastlines detailed, but the PUMAs themselves are quite small with their own unique borders. We can zoom in on the area around Chicago to see just how detailed these get. We've selected slightly different languages for each area to highlight unique distributions, like the relatively large number of Polish speakers in the Chicago metro area.

```
puma_by_langauge |>
  filter(language %in% c("chinese", "spanish", "polish")) |>
  fill_pumas() |>
  inner_join(PUMA, by = c("year" = "YEAR",
                          "location" = "location",
                          "PUMA" = "PUMA")) |>
  correct_projection() |>
  ggplot() +
```

**Proportion of non–English speakers by language**
in the Chicago area by PUMA

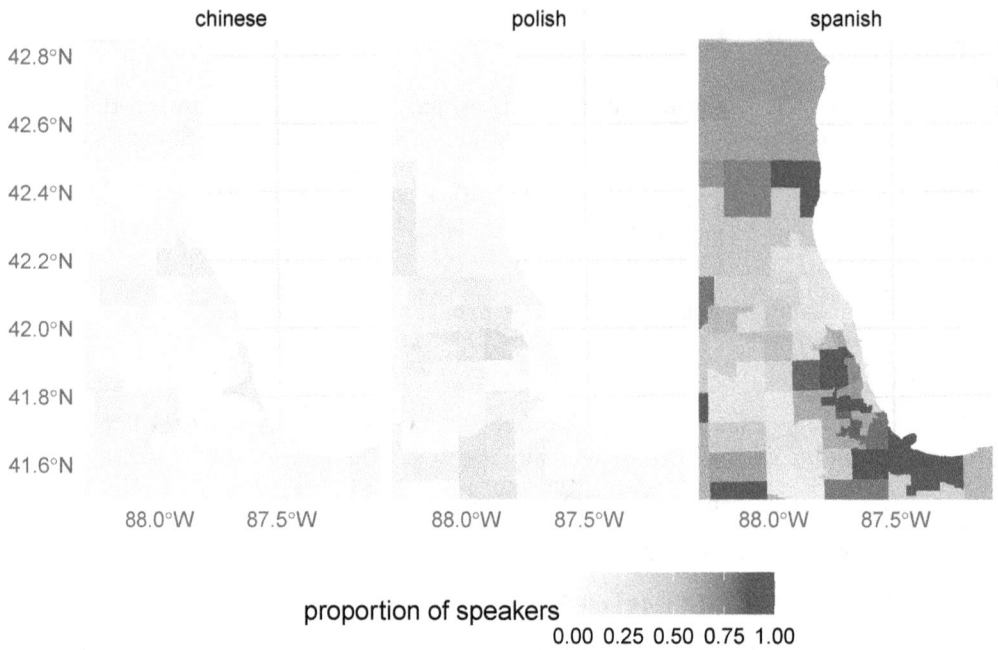

Figure 7.8: Proportion of speakers whose primary language is not English in the Chicago by PUMA, for Chinese, Polish, and Spanish

```
geom_sf(aes(geometry = geometry, fill = prop_speaker),
        lwd = 0) +
coord_sf(
  xlim = c(000000, 100000),
  ylim = c(000000, 150000),
  crs = "+proj=laea +lon_0=-88.3 +lat_0=41.5",
  expand = FALSE
) +
facet_wrap(vars(language), ncol = 3) +
scale_fill_distiller(type = "seq", direction = 1,
                     palette = "Greys",
                     name = "proportion of speakers") +
theme_minimal() +
theme(legend.position = "bottom") +
labs(
  title = "Proportion of non-English speakers by language",
  subtitle = "in the Chicago area by PUMA"
)
```

Or the Northeast, where there are a relatively large proportion of Portugese speakers in Massachusetts, and French speakers in Northern Maine.

```
puma_by_langauge |>
  filter(language %in% c("chinese", "spanish", "french",
                         "portuguese")) |>
  fill_pumas() |>
  inner_join(PUMA, by = c("year" = "YEAR",
                          "location" = "location",
                          "PUMA" = "PUMA")) |>
  correct_projection() |>
  ggplot() +
  geom_sf(aes(geometry = geometry, fill = prop_speaker),
          lwd = 0) +
  coord_sf(
    xlim = c(000000, 650000),
    ylim = c(000000, 810000),
    crs = "+proj=laea +lon_0=-74.5 +lat_0=40.4",
    expand = FALSE
  ) +
  facet_wrap(vars(language), ncol = 4) +
  scale_fill_distiller(type = "seq", direction = 1,
                       palette = "Greys", name =
                         "proportion of speakers") +
  theme_minimal() +
  theme(legend.position = "bottom") +
  labs(
    title = "Proportion of non-English speakers by language",
    subtitle = "in the Northeast"
  )
```

## 7.6 Summary

This chapter explored advanced topics for working with the arrow R package. We began talking about user-defined functions (UDFs), explaining how to create and utilize them to handle functions not natively supported by Arrow. We also looked at the interoperability between Arrow and DuckDB, showing how to use DuckDB for tasks not natively supported in Arrow. Finally, we took a look at extending arrow, with a focus on geospatial data, introducing the concept of GeoParquet for on-disk geospatial data representation that can quickly and easily be turned into an in-memory representation.

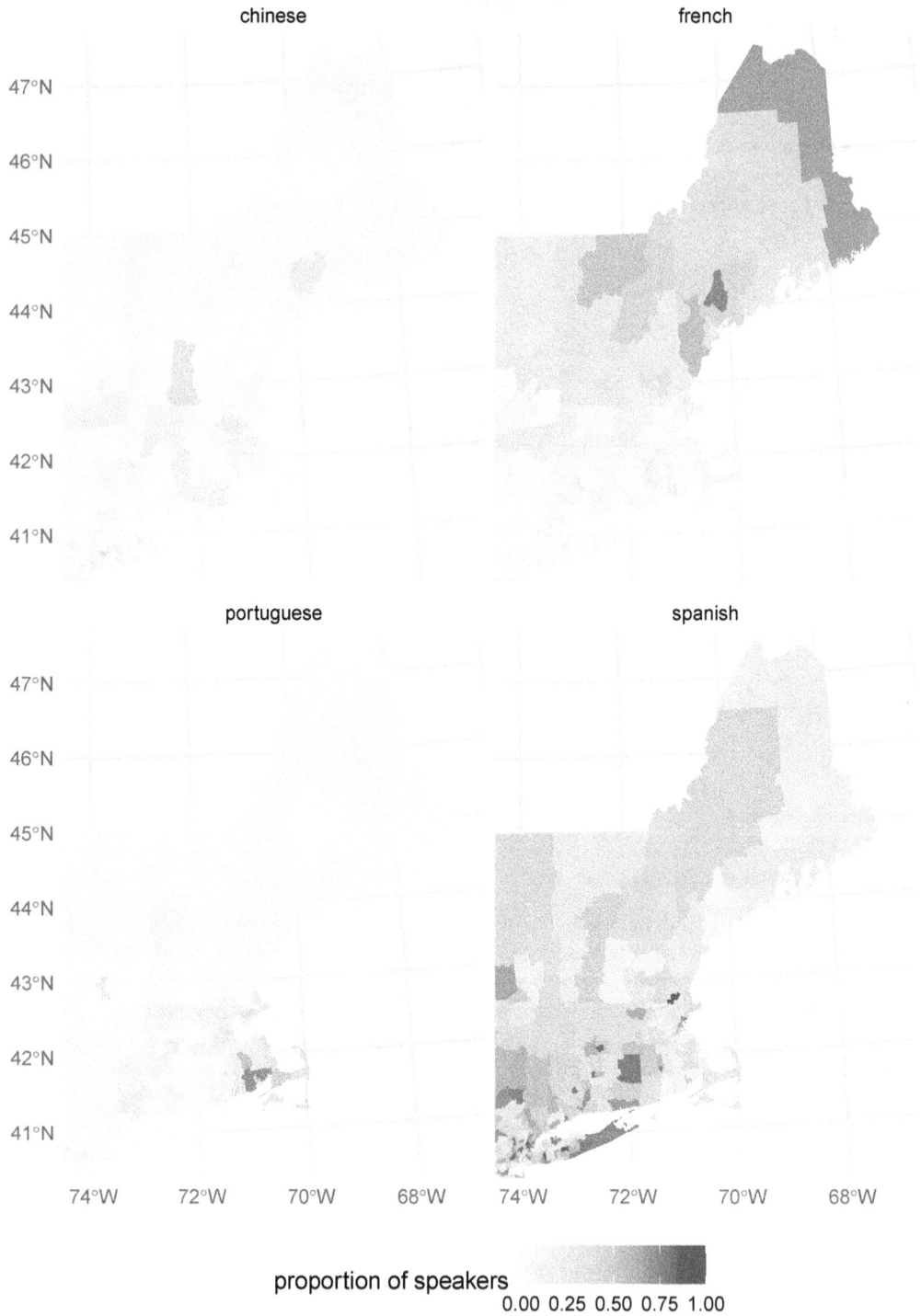

Figure 7.9: Proportion of speakers whose primary language is not English in the Northeast, by PUMA

# 8

# Sharing Data and Interoperability

One of the benefits of Arrow as a standard is that data can be easily shared between different applications or libraries that understand the format. By not having to convert to an intermediate format, and by avoiding serialization and deserialization costs, moving data from one tool to another is fast and efficient. As a library developer, it also reduces maintenance burden and the surface area for bugs because you don't have to write and manage adapters for many formats: you just implement the Arrow connector.

As a result, many projects have adopted the Arrow format as the way to connect with other projects in the ecosystem. In this chapter, we'll show some examples where Arrow is used as the means of exchanging data and how that results in major speedups for users. In some cases, Arrow is being used behind the scenes, and you benefit without needing to write any additional code.

Along the way, we'll highlight the different ways in which these different tools communicate—within the same process, across processes on the same system, or over the network between systems—and provide some context for how Arrow works in those modalities. Some of those details will be most relevant if you're trying to write a new library using Arrow, such as a new R package wrapping an Arrow-native project. But, even if you're not writing packages, developing an understanding of how arrow is communicating with other tools is useful for having an intuition about how it will perform in different contexts.

## 8.1   Sharing within a process

We've shown in Section 7.4 how you can pass data from the arrow query engine to duckdb and back. Let's explore a little more deeply how that works in order to understand what's happening and how the Arrow standard makes that basically free in terms of data copying costs.

Processes work on data by allocating memory and loading data into it. By allocating the memory, they ask the operating system to grant it ownership over a block of memory. Code running within a process can reference memory that the process has allocated, but other processes are not allowed to access it.

The integration between arrow and duckdb takes advantage of the fact that both are running in the same process. In your R session, arrow and duckdb are R packages that wrap C++ libraries. When you load the R packages, the C++ libraries are also loaded into the running R process. That means that a pointer to a block of memory that a function from the arrow library has created can be accessed by a function in the duckdb library just where it is: no need to copy or move anything, just read it from where it is.

DOI: 10.1201/9781032663197-8

However, we can't just pass C++ objects around. C++ objects are complex and include methods—methods that require code in the C++ library to execute. In order for DuckDB to work with an Arrow C++ object, it would have to depend on the Arrow C++ library, and vice versa. This is not desirable, and some features of C++[1] make this particularly challenging. Instead, we just want to pass the data buffer inside the C++ object. We only need a basic way to communicate where the data is and what its shape is. This is where the C data interface comes in.

## 8.1.1   The C data interface

The **Arrow C data interface** defines a simple means for referencing Arrow data in memory, allowing different libraries to consume the same data without depending on each other. It defines just two structures: one for an array of data and another for a schema. It is a small amount of C code—29 lines in total—so any programming language that is compatible with C can use it by copying this code into their codebase.

This can be a huge advantage to projects which utilize Arrow's format and data structures. For one, it's very small, so there's little cost to adding it. It avoids the need to bring in all of the dependencies of the Arrow C++ library, which may not be needed when you just want to exchange data in the Arrow format. Finally, the C data interface is stable. While the Arrow C++ library is under active development, the Arrow C data interface is guaranteed to remain unchanged.

## 8.1.2   Between R and Python

Before we explain how arrow and duckdb share data between the query engines, let's start with a simpler case that also uses the C data interface: sharing Arrow memory between R and Python with the **reticulate** package.

If you're working on a polyglot team which has people working both in R and in Python, or a project with both R and Python components, different components of your analysis pipeline might be in different languages. Passing data back and forth between the two— serialization and deserialization—can take time and resources, and so it's desirable to be able to avoid this if possible.

The reticulate R package already provides a way of passing data between R and Python in the same process, but it is not as efficient as using arrow. Let's take a look at two examples of passing data from R to Python and then returning it to R. In the first example, we'll work with use the standard method of passing data between these processes, and in our second example, we'll see how using Arrow speeds things up.

```
library(reticulate)
```

```
virtualenv_create("pyarrow-env")
install_pyarrow("pyarrow-env")
py_install("pandas", "pyarrow-env")
use_virtualenv("pyarrow-env")
```

First, let's make a data frame in memory of the data for Washington state.

---

[1] https://en.wikipedia.org/wiki/Name_mangling#C++

```
washington <- open_dataset("./data/person") |>
  filter(location == "wa") |>
  collect()
```

Because we called `collect()` on our data pipeline, the `washington` object is in memory as an R data frame. We'll send it to Python using `reticulate::r_to_py()`, then back to R with `py_to_r()`. In a real world example, you wouldn't just go back and forth: there would be some work you're doing in Python that requires you to switch to it. For this example though, we are only doing the round trip to show the cost of that part alone.

We need to have the pandas Python library loaded, so that the data can be passed to Python as a pandas table, otherwise it'll be passed as a Python dictionary object.

```
pd <- import("pandas")
```

```
returned_data <- washington |>
  r_to_py() |>
  py_to_r()
```

This took about 26 seconds when we ran it, due to reticulate needing to take the R data frame, convert it into the equivalent Python structure, a pandas DataFrame, and then convert it back to an R data frame.

Let's see how that looks using Arrow. By calling `compute()` at the end of our pipeline instead of `collect()`, we keep the result of the query in a table, not an R data frame.

```
pa <- import("pyarrow")
```

```
washington_table <- open_dataset("./data/person") |>
  filter(location == "wa") |>
  compute()
```

```
returned_arrow_data <- washington_table |>
  r_to_py() |>
  py_to_r()
```

This time it only took 0.2 seconds, which was a huge speed-up! How does this work?

Unlike in the first case, where data in R had to be copied and translated into a pandas DataFrame, here we used the Arrow C data interface to pass to Python the pointer to where the Arrow Table is stored in memory, and Python can use this to work with the table directly. The result in Python is a pyarrow Table. Naturally, the same happens when the data is passed back from Python to R. So, there is no conversion of data and copying data around: there is only a handoff of ownership.

### 8.1.3 DuckDB

The integration between arrow and duckdb builds on this machinery to share data between the query engines. Both DuckDB and Acero, the Arrow C++ query engine, operate on chunks of data at a time. This allows them to parallelize across multiple threads and efficiently stream results from one stage in the query evaluation to the next. Each stage, or node, including the data source node, behaves like an iterator: the next node of the query requests a batch of data from the previous one, and when it finishes processing it, it requests the next batch, until there are no more batches left.

In the Arrow C++ library, and thus also in R, this iterator is represented as a `RecordBatchReader`. To integrate with DuckDB, we deal in RecordBatchReaders: `to_duckdb()` hands off a reader to duckdb, and `to_arrow()` receives one back from duckdb. This works using an extension to the Arrow C data interface, the C data stream. The C object contains a reference to a callback function, which the consumer calls to request the next batch of data. As a result, batches of data can flow from one query engine to the other, almost as if they were a single engine.

Let's take a look at how this would work. The example below is a variation on the one we started the book with: we are finding the mean commute time by year, though this time we want this in hours instead of minutes and we aren't breaking it down by mode of transport.

```
pums_person <- open_dataset("./data/person")

commute_by_mode <- pums_person |>
  select(JWMNP, PWGTP, year) |>
  mutate(JWMNP_hours = JWMNP / 60) |>
  group_by(year) |>
  summarize(
    mean_commute_time = sum(JWMNP_hours * PWGTP, na.rm = TRUE) /
      sum(PWGTP, na.rm = TRUE),
    n_commuters = sum(PWGTP, na.rm = TRUE),
    .groups = "drop"
  ) |>
  collect()
```

With a query entirely in arrow, it takes 3.6 seconds to complete.

Now, to demonstrate the efficiency of swapping between arrow and duckdb we will send data to duckdb only for the minutes to hour mutation. Swapping back and forth for a mutation like this that arrow can do itself isn't something we would do in the real world, but it helps demonstrate how efficiently we can do the same calculations but passing the data back and forth.

```
pums_person <- open_dataset("./data/person")

commute_by_mode <- pums_person |>
  select(JWMNP, PWGTP, year) |>
  to_duckdb() |>
  mutate(JWMNP_hours = JWMNP / 60) |>
  to_arrow() |>
  group_by(year) |>
  summarize(
    mean_commute_time = sum(JWMNP_hours * PWGTP, na.rm = TRUE) /
      sum(PWGTP, na.rm = TRUE),
    n_commuters = sum(PWGTP, na.rm = TRUE),
    .groups = "drop"
  ) |>
  collect()
```

And going to duckdb for the mutation and then back to arrow for the rest, this takes only 4.5 seconds to complete. There is a small amount of overhead, but nowhere near as much as you would see if we had to serialize to a CSV, or even a Parquet file to pass data back and forth.

This example is contrived specifically to show the low overhead of passing data back and forth. In the real world, there would be no reason to pass data to duckdb when you can do the computation in arrow and vice versa. But this is extremely helpful if you're working in arrow and duckdb—or another library that can speak arrow—has a function that arrow doesn't.

---

## 8.2 Apache Spark integration: sharing across processes

In the previous section, we talked about sharing data within an individual system process, but what about if we want to share between separate processes? Different processes can't share memory: they have to allocate their own memory and share data with each other by sending messages. This introduces overhead, both in having to allocate memory for the copy of the data, and in encoding and decoding the message: our friends serialization and deserialization again.

As you may expect by now, Arrow provides a means to minimize that overhead. A great example of the benefits of using Arrow to communicate across systems is with Apache Spark. Speeding up data access with Spark was one of the initial use cases that demonstrated the value of Arrow. The first blog post[2] illustrating the benefits, focused on PySpark, is from 2017; an R version with **sparklyr**[3] came out in 2019. Both examples show speedups on the order of 20-40x, depending on the workflow.

Without Arrow, Spark had to send data one row at a time, serialized to a less efficient format, and then on the receiving side, pandas or R would have to reconstruct the data frame from the records. Sending data back to Spark did the same thing in reverse. As the benchmarks demonstrate, switching between row and column layouts is costly. With Arrow, data can stay in a columnar format, with less copying and transformation.

However, because we aren't running Spark in the same process, and likely not even on the same machine, we can't just point to a block of memory and start working with it, as we did with the C data interface. This is where Arrow's interprocess communication (IPC) format comes in. We've already seen this, in fact: it's the "Arrow file format". But it doesn't have to be written to a file; the important aspect is that it is fully encapsulated and can be sent from one process or system to another.

Similar to the C data interface for intraprocess communication, the IPC format is almost exactly the shape of the data in memory, so the serialization cost is near-zero. But unlike communicating within the same process, there is some cost to sending or receiving: you need to read it from disk or send it over the network, and allocate the memory to hold it.

A nice feature of the sparklyr integration in R is that you as the user don't need to change your analysis code to take advantage of it. All you have to do is load `library(arrow)`. If the arrow R package is loaded, sparkylr will use arrow for data transfer automatically.

---

[2]https://arrow.apache.org/blog/2017/07/26/spark-arrow/
[3]https://arrow.apache.org/blog/2019/01/25/r-spark-improvements/

## 8.3   Nanoarrow

Since Arrow has become the standard for columnar data, it is easier to integrate databases and data products with R. Rather than having to implement an adapter for the product's custom format, you can just use Arrow to connect with it. However, as this book shows, the arrow R package does a lot of things. If you just need to bring Arrow data into an R data frame, you don't need all of arrow's cloud file systems, its Parquet reader, the query engine, and other features.

This is where **nanoarrow**[4] comes in. The nanoarrow R package wraps just the C data interface and the IPC file format. It has packaged versions in R, Python, C, and C++. The R package supports translating Arrow data to and from R data frames, and that's about it. While it lacks a lot of the features of the full arrow R package, this is exactly the point: to create a minimal interface which allows users to be able to work with Arrow data structures in a small library.

While nanoarrow is relatively new, some R packages already use it. The **polars**[5] package, for example, uses nanoarrow to bring Arrow format data into R from the Polars data frame library—which is built on an implementation of Arrow in Rust. Similarly, **tiledb**[6] uses nanoarrow to bring Arrow data into R without require a dependency on the full arrow R package.

The nanoarrow project is a great example of how Arrow improves the experience of working with data. We have focused in this book on the arrow R package and the many ways it can be useful. But the Apache Arrow project and mission of improving the foundations for data analysis is much bigger than one package. Even when you aren't using the arrow R package itself, Arrow may be there behind the scenes, making your life easier.

## 8.4   Looking ahead

The list of examples of using Arrow to speed up data interchage is large, and it's still growing. Particularly as Arrow becomes more central to the internal workings of databases and query engines, we expect to see more projects using Arrow in R in more ways.

One promising direction is in getting data out of databases. For decades, the predominant standard in communicating with databases has been ODBC, which specifies how database drivers should receive SQL queries and return data. Both ODBC and JDBC, a similar standard that is implemented in Java, are row-oriented APIs, which as we have seen in previous chapters, means that there is a conversion step required to get into R's column-oriented data structures. This is further costly when the database that you are querying is also columnar—data is converted from columns to rows and then back to columns.

The Arrow project has defined a new standard called **ADBC**[7]. It is an API for communicating with databases that sends and receives Arrow-formatted data. By writing database

---

[4] https://arrow.apache.org/nanoarrow/latest/

[5] https://pola-rs.github.io/r-polars/

[6] https://tiledb-inc.github.io/TileDB-R/

[7] https://arrow.apache.org/blog/2023/01/05/introducing-arrow-adbc/

drivers that conform to the ADBC interface, getting data in and out of databases can be made more efficient and easier to work with on the client side. At the time of writing this book, ADBC has only begun to see adoption, but it has the potential to greatly improve the performance of querying databases.

A related area of interest is Arrow **Flight RPC**[8], a framework for high-performance across-network transfer. This is an alternative to sending messages over regular HTTP and is designed to maximize network throughput. ADBC database drivers could be implemented using Flight, or it could be used in custom data services. In principle, the integration with Spark could be further accelerated if it switched from sending Arrow IPC files to using Flight. As with ADBC, Flight is not yet widely adopted, but it holds promise for the future.

---

[8]https://arrow.apache.org/blog/2019/10/13/introducing-arrow-flight/

# A

# *Appendix*

## A.1 Package versions

Many R packages are under active development and occasionally updates can cause changes in compatibility. We've included the output of `sessionInfo()` so you can see the exact versions of the packages which were used to create the examples in this book.

```
sessionInfo()
```

```
R version 4.4.1 (2024-06-14)
Platform: x86_64-pc-linux-gnu
Running under: Ubuntu 22.04.4 LTS

Matrix products: default
BLAS:   /usr/lib/x86_64-linux-gnu/blas/libblas.so.3.10.0
LAPACK: /usr/lib/x86_64-linux-gnu/lapack/liblapack.so.3.10.0

locale:
 [1] LC_CTYPE=en_GB.UTF-8       LC_NUMERIC=C
 [3] LC_TIME=en_GB.UTF-8        LC_COLLATE=en_GB.UTF-8
 [5] LC_MONETARY=en_GB.UTF-8    LC_MESSAGES=en_GB.UTF-8
 [7] LC_PAPER=en_GB.UTF-8       LC_NAME=C
 [9] LC_ADDRESS=C               LC_TELEPHONE=C
[11] LC_MEASUREMENT=en_GB.UTF-8 LC_IDENTIFICATION=C

time zone: Europe/London
tzcode source: system (glibc)

attached base packages:
[1] stats     graphics  grDevices utils     datasets  methods
[7] base

other attached packages:
[1] dplyr_1.1.4            arrow_17.0.0.100000267

loaded via a namespace (and not attached):
 [1] vctrs_0.6.5       cli_3.6.3         knitr_1.47
 [4] rlang_1.1.4       xfun_0.45         purrr_1.0.2
 [7] generics_0.1.3    assertthat_0.2.1  jsonlite_1.8.8
[10] glue_1.7.0        bit_4.0.5         htmltools_0.5.8.1
[13] fansi_1.0.6       rmarkdown_2.27    tibble_3.2.1
```

DOI: 10.1201/9781032663197-A

```
[16] evaluate_0.24.0    fastmap_1.2.0     yaml_2.3.8
[19] lifecycle_1.0.4    compiler_4.4.1    pkgconfig_2.0.3
[22] rstudioapi_0.16.0 digest_0.6.36     R6_2.5.1
[25] tidyselect_1.2.1   utf8_1.2.4        pillar_1.9.0
[28] magrittr_2.0.3     tools_4.4.1       bit64_4.0.5
```

You can find even more detailed information about your arrow build by calling the function `arrow_info()`, which prints out information about which version of the Arrow R package and Arrow C++ library you have installed.

It also provides information about which features the Arrow C++ library has enabled when built, and so if you're using a custom Arrow build, it can help you check you've got everything you need.

The output below shows information about the version of Arrow used to build this book.

```
arrow_info()

Arrow package version: 17.0.0.100000267

Capabilities:

acero      TRUE
dataset    TRUE
substrait  FALSE
parquet    TRUE
json       TRUE
s3         TRUE
gcs        TRUE
utf8proc   TRUE
re2        TRUE
snappy     TRUE
gzip       TRUE
brotli     TRUE
zstd       TRUE
lz4        TRUE
lz4_frame  TRUE
lzo        FALSE
bz2        TRUE
jemalloc   TRUE
mimalloc   TRUE

Memory:

Allocator  mimalloc
Current    512 bytes
Max         64 Kb

Runtime:

SIMD Level          avx2
Detected SIMD Level avx2
```

Build:

```
C++ Library Version   18.0.0-SNAPSHOT
C++ Compiler                      GNU
C++ Compiler Version           11.4.0
```

## A.2   Getting started

### A.2.1   PUMS dataset overview

One of the datasets we use throughout this book is the United States of America's Census Public Access Microdata dataset. This is a dataset that comes from a detailed survey that is sent out to a subset of US residents every year. The dataset is release for public use by the Census Bureau in a raw CSV form. We have cleaned it up and converted it to a Parquet-based dataset for use with Arrow for demonstration purposes in this book.

We chose this data because it is open access, somewhat familiar, but also large and diverse in scope. Most analyses using PUMS will filter to a single year, a single state, or specific variables to be able to run analyses in memory. And then if you want to run the same analysis on a different year or different state, you would run the same code again on a different subset and then compare together. With the power of the arrow R package and datasets, we can analyze the full dataset with all of the available years and states.

#### A.2.1.1   Getting the data

We offer a few different ways that you can get the data that we use in this book. There are tradeoffs to each, but they each should get you enough data to run the examples, even if it's not the entire full dataset.

*A.2.1.1.1   Get a subset dataset*

When writing the book, we found it useful to have a small version of the dataset to test our code against. We have this dataset hosted in the GitHub repository under the releases: https://github.com/arrowrbook/book/releases

This subset only includes the person-level data for years 2005, 2018, and 2021 and only for states Alaska, Alabama, Arkansas, Arizona, California, Washington, Wisconsin, West Virginia, and Wyoming.

Simply download it and unzip it into a directory called **data** in your working directory and you can run the examples in this book.

*A.2.1.1.2   Download a full version from AWS S3*

We also host a full version of the dataset in AWS S3. However, we have set this bucket to have the person who requests the download to pay for the transfer cost. This means that you cannot download the data without first creating an AWS account, configuring it, and you will be billed a very small amount for the cost of the data transfer. The way to configure this in AWS might change, but the AWS documentation[1] have instructions for how to do this.

Once you have setup your AWS account and CLI[2], download the data into a `data` directory to use:

```
aws s3 cp --request-payer requester --recursive \
  s3://scaling-arrow-pums/ ./data/
```

This is the full dataset the book was built with, but does require that you setup an AWS account, configure it correctly, and pay the small transfer fee.

*A.2.1.1.3  Download the raw data from the Census Bureau and record it yourself*

We also have scripts that will download the raw data from the Census Bureau and do the recoding we started. Follow the instructions in the `README.md`[3] file under `pums_dataset` in the github repository. There are also scripts for downloading the shape files PUMA_shp_to_parquet.py[4].

There are a few variables you should set, and you can control the amount of parallelism for downloading, unzipping, etc.

This is the full dataset the book was built with, but does require computational time to finish.

### A.2.1.2  Dataset recoding

This dataset is a re-coding and enriching of the Public Use Microdata Sample (PUMS)[5] collected and provided by the United States Census. It covers years 2005–2022 using the 1-year estimates (though 2020 is missing since that year's was only released in 5-year estimates due to COVID).

The raw data was retrieved from the Census's FTP site[6] and the values to recode categorical and string data was retrieved from the Census's API (via the **censusapi** R package).

The data was recoded with the following general principles:

- If there were string values and there were less than or equal to 10 unique values, we converted these to factors.
- If there were string values and there were more than 10 unique values, we converted these to strings.
- We used integer or floats for values that were numeric in nature, and recoded special values (e.g. variable `RETP` "Retirement income past 12 months" where a value of −1 means "N/A (Less than 15 years old)") that are missing-like as `NA`. Note: there are also a number of values that are top and bottom coded—these are also converted to numerics (e.g. so a maximum value in those columns actually represents that value or larger; variable `WKHP` or "Usual hours worked per week past 12 months" which has a value of 99 marked as "99 Or More Usual Hours").

---

[1] https://docs.aws.amazon.com/AmazonS3/latest/userguide/ObjectsinRequesterPaysBuckets.html
[2] https://docs.aws.amazon.com/cli/latest/userguide/getting-started-quickstart.html
[3] https://github.com/arrowrbook/book/blob/main/pums_dataset/README.md
[4] https://github.com/arrowrbook/book/blob/main/pums_dataset/PUMA_shp_to_parquet.py
[5] https://www.census.gov/programs-surveys/acs/microdata.html
[6] https://www2.census.gov/programs-surveys/acs/data/pums/

- If there were codes that broadly corresponded to `TRUE` and `FALSE` (e.g. "yes" and "no"), these were converted into booleans

The book *Analyzing US Census Data: Methods, Maps, and Models in R*[7] has chapters dedicated to analyzing this kind of microdata[8] with **tidycensus** package. Though the tidycensus package and approach will have slight differences from analyzing this data with arrow, the concepts and analytic approach will be the same.

Though we have not purposefully altered this data, this data should not be relied on to be a perfect or even possibly accurate representation of the official PUMS dataset.

### A.2.1.3   Datasets and partitioning

There are two datasets, one at `s3://scaling-arrow-pums/person/` which has person-level data and another at `s3://scaling-arrow-pums/household/` which has household-level data.

Each of these datasets is subsequently partitioned by year and then by state/territory with prefixes like `year=2019/location=il` with Parquet files below that.

### A.2.1.4   Using the PUMS dataset

A detailed description of how to analyze PUMS or other survey data is beyond the scope of this book, though if you're interested in learning more details, the book Analyzing US Census Data: Methods, Maps, and Models in R[9] has chapters dedicated to analyzing this kind of microdata[10]. But it's helpful to explore some examples.

The PUMS dataset comes from surveying around 1% of the US population. It also asks a number of sensitive questions, so the Census Bureau is careful to avoid accidentally identifying specific people in the dataset. For these two reasons, the dataset is actually not the raw responses—where each row is one respondent—but rather each row has a specific weight applied to it. This weight could be thought of as something along the lines of "this number of respondents responded with this set of answers" though it is more complicated than that. Because of this, in order to make estimates about populations, we need to use the weighting columns from the dataset which tell us how many people are represented in each row to get an accurate measure in our final calculations which is different from a typical tidy workflow where each row is a single individual and you can use simple aggregations across rows.

In sum, this dataset uses survey weights, so the individual rows do not represent a single individual. Instead, we must use the weight columns if we are counting people or calculating many statistics (measures of central tendency especially).

Let's look at an example, if we are doing an age breakdown for the state of Alaska, we might think we could do simply:

```
pums_person |>
  filter(location == "ak") |>
  mutate(
    age_group = case_when(
      AGEP < 25 ~ "24 and under",
      AGEP < 35 ~ "25-34",
```

---

[7] https://walker-data.com/census-r/index.html

[8] https://walker-data.com/census-r/introduction-to-census-microdata.html

[9] https://walker-data.com/census-r/index.html

[10] https://walker-data.com/census-r/introduction-to-census-microdata.html

```
      AGEP < 45 ~ "35-44",
      AGEP < 55 ~ "45-54",
      AGEP < 65 ~ "55-64",
      TRUE ~ "65+"
    )
  ) |>
  group_by(year, age_group) |>
  summarize(num_people = n()) |>
  arrange(year, age_group) |>
  collect()
```

```
# A tibble: 102 x 3
# Groups:   year [17]
     year age_group      num_people
    <int> <chr>               <int>
 1   2005 24 and under        2366
 2   2005 25-34                676
 3   2005 35-44                915
 4   2005 45-54               1041
 5   2005 55-64                637
 6   2005 65+                  494
 7   2006 24 and under        2433
 8   2006 25-34                713
 9   2006 35-44                891
10   2006 45-54               1084
# i 92 more rows
```

Looking at the results here is off, the numbers look way too low. If we add up the total of all age groups for 2021, we get: 6,411 which is far under the estimates of the 2021 population of 732,673.

But if we instead sum the person weight column (PWGTP) we get very different results:

```
pums_person |>
  filter(location == "ak") |>
  mutate(
    age_group = case_when(
      AGEP < 25 ~ "24 and under",
      AGEP < 35 ~ "25-34",
      AGEP < 45 ~ "35-44",
      AGEP < 55 ~ "45-54",
      AGEP < 65 ~ "55-64",
      TRUE ~ "65+"
    )
  ) |>
  group_by(year, age_group) |>
  summarize(num_people = sum(PWGTP)) |>
  arrange(year, age_group) |>
  collect()
```

```
# A tibble: 102 x 3
# Groups:   year [17]
```

```
   year age_group    num_people
   <int> <chr>          <int>
1  2005 24 and under    265268
2  2005 25-34            76200
3  2005 35-44           101715
4  2005 45-54           108320
5  2005 55-64            65431
6  2005 65+              41068
7  2006 24 and under    254235
8  2006 25-34            89767
9  2006 35-44            98676
10 2006 45-54           109716
# i 92 more rows
```

And here, if we do our sum for 2021 again, we get a number that matches the overall population for Alaska in 2021: 732,673.

## A.2.2 Arrow data types

In the introduction, we mentioned that Arrow is designed for interoperability between different systems, and provides a standard for how to represent tabular data. In order to achieve this interoperability, Arrow defines a set of data types which cover the main data types used in different data systems. These data types are similar to those used in R but are not identical. In R, you may have previously encountered:

- integers (e.g. `1L`)
- numeric (e.g. `1.1`)
- complex (e.g. `1 + 1i`)
- character (e.g. `"a"`)
- factors (e.g. `factor("a")`)
- logical (e.g. `TRUE`)
- other types relating to dates, times of day, and durations

Arrow data types are similar to these, but some are more precise and also include some data types which don't exist in R. The Arrow data types are:

- **integers**: Arrow has multiple integer types which vary on whether they are signed—if they can be both positive and negative, or just positive—and how much space in memory they take up
- **floating point** numbers: these map to numeric values, and vary on how much space in memory they take up
- **decimal** numbers: these use integers to represent non-integer data with exact precision, to allow for more precise arithmetic
- **utf8** and **binary**: similar to R's character vectors
- **dictionaries**: similar to R factors
- **boolean**: equivalent to R logical values
- **datetimes** and **dates**
- **durations**
- **time** of day

### A.2.2.1  Bit-width sizes

Another aspect of these Arrow data types is that some of them can come in different sizes. For example, integers can be 8, 16, 32, or 64 bits. They can also be signed (can be positive of negative) or unsigned (only positive). The size of an integer refers to how much space it takes up in memory, and the practical impact of this is the range of values it can hold. Eight-bit values can take up $2^8$ bits, which comes to 256. This means that an unsigned 8-bit integer can be any value between 0 and 255, and a signed 8-bit integer can be any value between $-128$ and 127.

There is a trade-off between the number of bits and the size of numbers that can be represented. For example, if you have a column that never has values over 100, using an 8-bit integer would hold that data and be smaller than storing it in a column that is 16, 32, or 64 bits. However, if you have a have a column that frequently takes values up to ~10 billion, you're going to need to use a 64-bit integer.

You can find out more about the Arrow data types[11] by reading the project documentation[12], though for many people working with Arrow, you don't need to have a thorough understanding of these data types, as Arrow automatically converts between Arrow and R data types. If you don't have a specific reason to deviate from the default conversion, there's usually little benefit to doing so Switching from a 32-bit integer to an 8-bit integer won't lead to significant performance gains for most datasets, and optimizing for the best partitioning structure and storage format is much more important.

See Section A.2.2.3 and Section A.2.2.4 for more details about these conversions.

### A.2.2.2  Casting

If you want to convert from one Arrow data type to another, you can use casting in dplyr pipelines. For example, if we create a tibble with a column of integers, and convert it to an Arrow table, the default conversion creates a 32-bit integer.

```
tibble::tibble(x = 1:3) |>
  arrow_table()
```

```
Table
3 rows x 1 columns
$x <int32>
```

However, we can use `cast()` to convert it to a different bitwidth, in this example, a 64-bit integer.

```
tibble::tibble(x = 1:3) |>
  arrow_table() |>
  mutate(y = cast(x, int64()))
```

```
Table (query)
x: int32
y: int64 (cast(x, {to_type=int64, allow_int_overflow=false,
allow_time_truncate=false, allow_time_overflow=false,
allow_decimal_truncate=false, allow_float_truncate=false,
allow_invalid_utf8=false}))
```

---

[11] https://arrow.apache.org/docs/r/articles/data_types.html
[12] https://arrow.apache.org/docs/r

See $.data for the source Arrow object

### A.2.2.3 Translations from R to Arrow

Table A.1 is slightly modified from the Arrow project documentation[13], but clearly marks the mappings between R types and Arrow types.

Table A.1: R data types and their equivalent Arrow data types

| Original R type | Arrow type after translation |
| --- | --- |
| logical | boolean |
| integer | int32 |
| double ("numeric") | float64 [1] |
| character | utf8 [2] |
| factor | dictionary |
| raw | uint8 |
| Date | date32 |
| POSIXct | timestamp |
| POSIXlt | struct |
| data.frame | struct |
| list [3] | list |
| bit64::integer64 | int64 |
| hms::hms | time32 |
| difftime | duration |

[1]: The two types `float64` and `double` are the same in Arrow C++; however, only `float64()` is used in arrow since the function `double()` already exists in base R.

[2]: If the character vector is exceptionally large—over 2 GB of strings—it will be converted to a `large_utf8` Arrow type.

[3]: Only lists where all elements are the same type are able to be translated to Arrow list type (which is a "list of" some type). Arrow has a heterogeneous list type, but that is not exposed in the arrow R package.

### A.2.2.4 Converting from Arrow to R

Table A.2 shows Arrow types and the R types they are translated to.

---

[13] https://arrow.apache.org/docs/r/

Table A.2: Arrow data types and their equivalent R data types

| Original Arrow type | R type after translation |
|---|---|
| boolean | logical |
| int8 | integer |
| int16 | integer |
| int32 | integer |
| int64 | integer [1] |
| uint8 | integer |
| uint16 | integer |
| uint32 | integer [1] |
| uint64 | integer [1] |
| float16 | - [2] |
| float32 | double |
| float64 | double |
| utf8 | character |
| large_utf8 | character |
| binary | arrow_binary [3] |
| large_binary | arrow_large_binary [3] |
| fixed_size_binary | arrow_fixed_size_binary [3] |
| date32 | Date |
| date64 | POSIXct |
| time32 | hms::hms |
| time64 | hms::hms |
| timestamp | POSIXct |
| duration | difftime |
| decimal | double |
| dictionary | factor [4] |
| list | arrow_list [5] |
| large_list | arrow_large_list [5] |
| fixed_size_list | arrow_fixed_size_list [5] |
| struct | data.frame |
| null | vctrs::vctrs_unspecified |
| map | arrow_list [5] |
| union | - [2] |

[1]: These integer types may contain values that exceed the range of R's `integer` type (32 bit signed integer). When they do, `uint32` and `uint64` are converted to `double` ("numeric") and `int64` is converted to `bit64::integer64`. This conversion can be disabled (so that `int64` always yields a `bit64::integer64` vector) by setting `options(arrow.int64_downcast = FALSE)`.

[2]: Some Arrow data types do not currently have an R equivalent and will raise an error if cast to or mapped to via a schema.

[3]: `arrow*_binary` classes are implemented as lists of raw vectors.

[4]: Due to the limitation of R factors, Arrow `dictionary` values are coerced to string when translated to R if they are not already strings.

[5]: `arrow*_list` classes are implemented as subclasses of `vctrs_list_of` with a `ptype` attribute set to what an empty Array of the value type converts to.

## A.3  Cloud

### A.3.1  Network data transfer monitoring with nethogs

If you have a Linux machine and want to test the amount of data transferred to your machine while running similar examples to the ones found in this book, after installing nethogs, you can run the following code:

```
sudo nethogs -v 3
```

This runs the **nethogs** utility as a root user.

# *Index*

Note: Page numbers in *italics* represent figures; **bold** represent tables; n and number represent footnote and note number.

For Product Safety Concerns and Information please contact our EU
representative GPSR@taylorandfrancis.com
Taylor & Francis Verlag GmbH, Kaufingerstraße 24, 80331 München, Germany